Tax Facts 8

Tax Facts 8

by Isabella Horry
Filip Palda
Michael A. Walker

The Fraser Institute
Vancouver, British Columbia, Canada

Canadian Cataloguing in Publication Data

Horry, Isabella, 1963–
Tax Facts 8

First ed. published in 1976 under title: How much tax do you really pay?
Includes bibliographical references.
ISBN 0–88975–152–8

1. Taxation—Canada. 2. Tax incidence—
Canada. I. Palda, Filip (K. Filip). II.
Walker, Michael, 1945– III. Fraser
Institute (Vancouver, B.C.). IV. Title

HJ2451.H69 1992   336.2'00971   C92–091794–1
74878

Table of Contents

Chapter 7

Appendix

List of Tables and Figures

Tables

Appendix

Figures

Preface

THIS BOOK IS A SUMMARY of the latest results of a Fraser Institute project that began in July 1975. Its objective was to find out how much tax, in all forms, Canadians pay to federal, provincial, and municipal governments and how the size of this tax bill has changed over the years since 1961. In the interim, seven editions of this book have been published.

The series of books has been written with two distinct purposes in mind: first, to provide a non-technical do-it-yourself manual so the average Canadian family can estimate how much tax they pay; second, to update a statistic, first published in 1976, that we call the Canadian Consumer Tax Index. This index measures how much the tax bill of an average Canadian family has increased since 1961 and how much it is changing currently. In other words, it measures changes in the price that Canadians pay for government.

This book does not attempt to look at the benefits Canadians receive from government in return for their taxes. Rather, it looks at the price that is paid for a product—government. It has nothing to say about the quality of the product, how much of it each of us receives, or whether we get our money's worth. These questions are, however, considered in the Institute publication, *Government Spending Facts* which is a companion volume.

This year, for the first time, the statistics contained in this book are based on an analysis of the individual circumstances of some 41,000

Canadian taxpayers. In previous years the analysis was done with group average data pre-compiled by Statistics Canada. Because this year's analysis is built up from individual tax files, it is possible to examine the situation of particular kinds of taxpayers with a good deal more precision. This is reflected in the special tables in the appendix and also in the commentary provided in the text.

The Fraser Institute calculations of tax burden are part of an on-going program of research. In making these results available to the public, we seek both to inform and to be informed. Readers who disagree with our methods or conclusions are invited to write to the Institute to convey the nature of their reservations. In this way, our methods and our estimates can be refined and perfected.

— *Michael A. Walker*

Acknowledgements

WE ARE PLEASED TO ACKNOWLEDGE the assistance of Statistics Canada which provided certain unpublished background data essential to this study. The Canadian Tax Simulator computer programs were originally written by David Gill whose unsparing efforts we are pleased to acknowledge. The sixth and seventh editions have been computed on a set of programs modified to run on a micro-computer system. These modifications were completed by Douglas T. Wills who has gone on to climb other mountains. This edition of *Tax Facts* is computed using the SPSS statistical package for which the programming was done by Filip Palda and Isabella Horry.

About the Authors

Isabella D. Horry

Isabella D. Horry is a research economist with The Fraser Institute. She was born in Vancouver, Canada and attended the University of British Columbia receiving a Bachelor of Arts in economics in 1985 and a Master of Arts in economics in 1987. She joined The Fraser Institute in 1988, and co-authored *Tax Facts 6* (1988) and *Tax Facts 7* (1990) with Sally C. Pipes and Michael A. Walker and *Government Spending Facts* (1991) with Michael A. Walker. Isabella Horry is a member of the Association of Professional Economists of B.C.

Filip Palda

Filip Palda is Senior Economist at the Fraser Institute. Born in 1962 in Montreal, he received his B.A. in 1983 and M.A. in 1984, in economics, from Queen's University, and his Ph.D. in economics from the University of Chicago in 1989. His dissertation, "Electoral Spending" was supervised by Gary S. Becker. His specialties are the economic of elections, taxation, and development. He is author of numerous academic articles on development economics and public choice theory, which have appeared in *Economic Inquiry*, *Public Choice*, and *Journal des Economistes et des Etudes Humaines*. He also wrote The Fraser Institute book *Election Finance Regulation in Canada: A Critical Review*. He is a regular op-ed contributor to the Sterling chain of newspapers, frequently appears on radio and television, and is an expert witness in matters of election finance.

Michael A. Walker

Michael Walker is Director of The Fraser Institute. Born in Newfoundland in 1945, he received his B.A. (summa) at St. Francis Xavier University in 1966 and his Ph.D. in economics at the University of Western Ontario in 1969. From 1969 to 1973 he worked in various research capacities at the Bank of Canada, Ottawa, and when he left in 1973 was Research Officer in charge of the Special Studies and Monetary Policy Group in the Department of Banking. Immediately prior to joining The Fraser Institute, Dr. Walker was Econometric Model Consultant to the Federal Department of Finance, Ottawa. Dr. Walker has also taught Monetary Economics and Statistics at the University of Western Ontario and Carleton University.

Dr. Walker writes regularly for daily newspapers and financial periodicals. His articles have also appeared in technical journals, including the *Canadian Journal of Economics, Canadian Public Policy, Canadian Taxation* and the *Canadian Tax Journal.* He has been a columnist in *The Province,* the Toronto *Sun, The Ottawa Citizen, The Financial Post,* the Sterling newspaper chain, and community newspapers across Canada.

He is an author, editor, and contributor to more than twenty books on economic matters, some of which include *Balancing the Budget; Flat-Rate Tax Proposals; Reaction: The National Energy Program; Rent Control: A Popular Paradox; Unions and the Public Interest; Discrimination, Affirmative Action and Equal Opportunity; Privatization: Theory and Practice; Trade Unions and Society; Privatization: Tactics and Techniques;* and *Freedom, Democracy and Economic Welfare.*

Dr. Walker is a member of the Mont Pèlerin Society, the Canadian and American Economic Associations, and the International Association of Energy Economists.

Chapter 1

The Canadian Tax System

Canada in the world of 1992

IN THE 1970S ARTHUR LAFFER made popular an old piece of economic wisdom which held that if a government raised tax rates too high, tax collections might actually fall. Fear that the U.S. was on the "wrong side of the Laffer Curve" was behind President Reagan's promise to reform taxes. Studies since then suggest that almost no country is at the point where an increase in tax rates will lead to less tax collected. This problem, however, is no longer the central concern of governments. More subtle ideas now preoccupy policy-makers. Their main concern is how to design an "efficient" set of taxes: one that does not interfere with the types of decisions people make in the marketplace. We now know that taxes distort people's decisions, leading to market exchanges that leave opportunities for mutually beneficial exchanges unexploited.

A tax system that interferes too much with people's decisions can also cripple a nation's ability to compete with others. As free international trade becomes a reality, governments will be forced to fashion taxes to prevent the flight of people and resources. The record of the past eight years suggests that Canadian governments have yet to fully appreciate this lesson. Even though the Progressive Conservatives came to power in 1984 on a platform of government restraint and have managed to some degree to make the tax system more efficient, the federal income taxes of the average Canadian family have increased in real terms by $1,119 in 1992 dollars since 1984. The sum of all taxes has risen by $2,622 in 1992 dollars. Figure 1.1 charts the progress of taxes since 1984.

The many faces of the tax collector

What Figure 1.1 shows is that the Canadian tax system is continually changing. To understand current trends of change, it is important to understand how the Canadian system of taxation has evolved. Under the Canadian constitution, the federal government and the provincial governments are essentially given unlimited powers of taxation. In the British North America Act, the immediate predecessor of the Canadian

Figure 1.1:
Federal, Provincial, and Municipal Taxes Collected from the Average Canadian Family, 1984-1992 (in 1992 dollars)

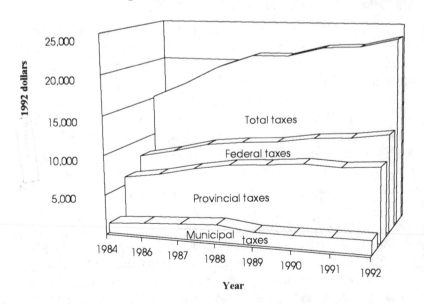

Source: Fraser Institute Canadian Tax Simulator (CANTASIM).

constitution, the provinces are limited to the collection of taxes which are paid directly by the person being taxed—so-called direct taxes. But because of the broad judicial interpretation given to the meaning of "direct," the provinces have been able to levy all sorts of taxes except import duties and taxes on sales which cross provincial borders. Given this unlimited scope for taxation and the 100 years of ingenuity that have elapsed, it is not surprising that Canada now has a very complicated tax system.[1]

Some understanding of this complexity can be obtained simply by noting the 15 categories of tax set out in Table 1.1. This number has grown over the past few years as new taxes, like those on energy, and the airport tax, have been implemented. During 1991 another major tax in the form of an extension of the federal sales tax, the Goods and Services Tax (G.S.T.), was visited on Canadians.

Income taxes predominate

Table 1.1 and Figure 1.2 show that personal income taxes are the largest single source of government revenue. During 1991 some 107.9 billion dollars were extracted by federal and provincial income tax—a sum which represented 42.7 percent of the total taxes that Canadians pay. Second in line as a source of federal and provincial revenues was the sales tax—representing 14.7 percent of tax revenue and 37.2 billion tax dollars. Corporate profits taxes, at 6.4 percent of total taxes, accounted for a further 16.2 billion dollars, while property and natural resource taxes accounted for 31.5 billion dollars and 12.5 percent collectively. Together these five kinds of tax accounted for nearly 76.3 percent of total government revenue during 1991. (Interestingly, both the corporate profits tax and the income tax were implemented in 1916 and 1917 as "temporary" measures to finance World War I.)

---

1   A survey of the evolution of the Canadian tax system with emphasis on the sharing of tax revenues between the provinces and the federal government can be found in Perrin Lewis' chapter, "The Tangled Tale of Taxes and Transfers," in M. Walker (editor), *Canadian Confederation at the Crossroads*, The Fraser Institute, 1979.

Table 1.1 also illustrates how the Canadian tax structure has evolved over the thirty years since 1961. The most obvious change has been the evolution of the personal income tax. While always a prominent feature

Table 1.1: The different taxes paid by Canadians and the proportion that they represent of the total

	1961		1991	
	$ millions	%	$ millions	%
Personal Income Taxes	2,099	22.7	107,930	42.7
General Sales Taxes	1,351	14.6	37,227	14.7
Health & Social Insurance Levies	663	7.2	25,252	10.0
Real Property Tax	1,285	13.9	21,181	8.4
Corporate Income Taxes	1,199	13.0	16,200	6.4
Liquor & Tobacco Taxes	837	9.1	9,714	3.2
Motive Fuel Taxes	525	5.7	8,061	3.2
Miscellaneous Taxes	55	0.6	6,950	2.7
Natural Resource Revenues	266	2.9	6,144	2.4
Privileges, Licences & Permits	190	2.1	4,635	1.8
Other Property & Related Taxes	150	1.6	4,195	1.7
Import Duties	438	4.7	4,055	1.6
Other Consumption Taxes	173	1.9	1,543	0.6
Non-residents	0	0.0	1,470	0.6
Petroleum & Natural Gas Revenues	0	0.0	0	0.0
Total	9,231	100.0	254,556	100.0

Source: Statistics Canada, catalogue nos. 68-211, 68-207, 68-204, and 68-512.

Figure 1.2
Where Governments Obtained their Revenue, 1961

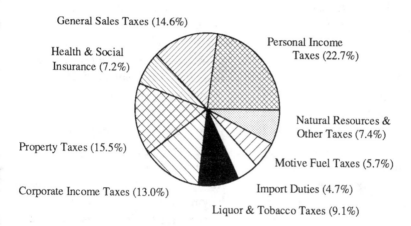

Where Governments Obtained their Revenue, 1991

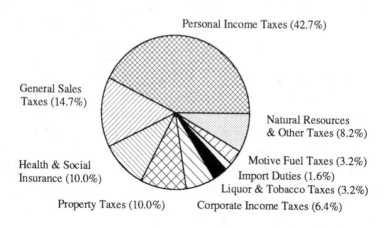

Source: See Table 1.1

of the tax system, the income tax has, in recent years, become increasingly important. In 1961 income taxes represented only 22.7 cents out of every tax dollar Canadians paid, but by 1991 income taxes accounted for 42.7 cents—nearly three times the revenue generated by the second-running sales tax.

This increase came about largely through passive interaction between the progressive income tax system and money incomes swollen by inflation.[2] Until the income tax was indexed to the inflation rate in 1974, all income increases were taxed at progressively higher rates in spite of the fact that much of the increased income represented illusory inflation-based gains.

As a consequence of this revenue growth, government was able to rely less on other forms of taxation and to allow the burden of some of these taxes to decrease. However, in some important cases—notably sales tax and resource taxes—the rate of tax was increased despite rapidly growing revenues from personal income tax. (Table 1.2 presents the burden of the top nine taxes contributing to government revenue in 1991. The figures in the table are the effective rates of taxation relative to total Canadian income.)

While revenue from the income tax explosion poured into the federal government's coffers, the provinces were led by their perceived need for tax revenue to gradually boost their sales tax rates (except for Alberta, which has no sales tax, and in British Columbia, where the sales tax has been adjusted up and down—it was reduced from 7 percent to 5 percent on April 11, 1978, on April 1, 1979 a further reduction to 4 percent was made. However, on March 10, 1981 it was increased to 6 percent and in July, 1983 to 7 percent. In the 1987 budget, the tax was once again dropped to 6 percent). The federal government also sought to increase its revenue from indirect sources, in the early and mid 1980s, by increasing its takings from the manufacturer's sales tax, and starting in 1991 by replacing this tax with the more comprehensive GST. Depart-

---

2   Douglas Hartle, "An Open Letter to Allen Lambert..." *The Financial Post*, Feb. 11, 1979. Mr. Hartle was a senior civil servant in the federal Treasury Board during the latter period of the income tax explosion.

TABLE 1.2:
Total taxes as a percentage of total Canadian income

	1961	1991
	Percent	
Personal Income Taxes	5.1%	15.9%
General Sales Taxes	3.3	5.5
Health & Social Insurance Levies	1.6	3.7
Property Tax	3.5	3.7
Corporate Income Taxes	2.9	2.4
Liquor & Tobacco Taxes	2.0	1.4
Import Duties	1.1	0.6
Motive Fuel Taxes	1.3	1.2
Natural Resources & Other Taxes	1.7	3.1
Total	22.6	37.5

Source: See table 1.1 and Statistics Canada catalogue 13-001.

ment of Finance officials hoped to raise an extra $10 billion annually from this new source.

The rise in resource taxation in the 1970s and 1980s resulted primarily from rises in the price of oil and gas, triggered by the oil embargo and subsequent cartelization of oil pricing by the OPEC countries in 1973.[3] In the normal course of events these price rises in Canada would automatically have meant a sharp rise in the return to Canadian producers. But the reaction of provincial governments was to absorb much of this "windfall," or "rent," as it has been called, in the form of higher taxes or royalties. The federal government, for its part, imposed a further tax on producers who were exporting oil. (This tax, the oil export charge, amounted to the difference between the controlled Canadian price per barrel and the world price.) Proceeds from the federal tax were then

---

3   For a complete discussion of oil pricing and taxation, see G.C. Watkins and M.A. Walker (editors), *Oil in the Seventies,* The Fraser Institute, 1977.

used to subsidize imports of foreign oil into the eastern Canadian provinces.

From 1974 to 1984 both the provincial and federal governments escalated their tax effort—but especially the federal government. The National Energy Program and the subsequent Energy Agreement allowed the federal government to earn about 4 billion dollars from petroleum during 1984.

The 1985 Federal budget incorporated a number of changes in regard to energy taxes agreed upon in the Western Accord with the governments of Saskatchewan, Alberta, and British Columbia. Both the oil export charge and petroleum compensation charge were eliminated. Other energy taxes, such as the Petroleum and Gas Revenue tax, were revised, reduced, and in some cases phased out. These changes combined with the decline in world oil prices has resulted in energy related revenues declining in both relative and absolute terms.

The late 1980s and early 1990s saw the federal government trying to make income, corporate, and sales taxes more efficient and less of a burden to the ability of Canadians to compete in the international marketplace. While corporate and income tax *rates* fell, many deductions were eliminated in order to expand the tax *base*. These changes were supposed to lessen the degree to which taxes enter into the decisions of Canadians. If this principle seems strange, consider a flat tax. Such a tax is not related to any economic activity in which the individual may engage. Government simply takes a fixed amount away. The government taking may be huge, but since the tax is not related to how much the individual works or spends, it will not directly affect his behaviour.

Lowering tax rates, however, did not lead to less tax collection.

In fact, in the past eight years the federal collections from the average family have risen by $1,519 in 1992 dollars. This rise is due to the expanding tax base. That the federal government has not collected even more taxes is due to its declining commitment to provincial projects such as welfare, education, and health care. In reaction, the provinces have chosen to make up the shortfall not by reducing spending, but by increasing their taxes.

The provinces have been able to raise provincial income taxes less visibly than the federal government because of the "tax-on-tax" system

Table 1.3: Provincial Income tax rate as a percentage of the basic federal income tax

	1986	1991
Newfoundland	60.0	62.0
P.E.I.	52.5	58.0
Nova Scotia	56.5	59.5
New Brunswick	58.0	60.0
Quebec	—	—
Ontario	50.0	53.0
Manitoba	54.0	52.0
Saskatchewan	50.0	50.0
Alberta	43.5	46.5
B.C.	47.5	51.5

Source: *The National Finances*, 1991; Canadian Tax Foundation, 1992.

in which all provinces except Quebec impose a tax upon the federal tax. Table 1.3 shows the tax rate each province imposes on the federal tax. The federal government collects the tax and returns it to the provinces. In what may have been an effort to dissociate itself from provincial tax collection practices, in 1991 the federal government questioned Canadians about how they would feel about filling out two income tax forms: one for Ottawa and one for their province. This idea is still in its early stages.

Dividing the spoils

Determining which level of government will get how much revenue is one of the important tax questions of the 1990s. Table 1.4 and Figure 1.2 provide a breakdown of major taxes by federal, provincial, and municipal levels of government for the years 1961 and 1991. Total taxes collected now amount to 37.5 cents out of every dollar of GDP, a 65 percent rise since 1961. Provincial governments are rapidly becoming the dominant tax collectors. In 1961 provincial governments collected

31.9 percent of total taxes in Canada, while federal and municipal governments collected 68.1 percent. By 1991, however, provincial governments were collecting 40.5 percent and the other levels only 59.5 percent.

It must be acknowledged that the impression given by these figures is distorted somewhat by the fact that some of the revenue of municipal and provincial governments comes from other levels of government. For example, in 1961 fully 30 percent of provincial and municipal revenues were derived from other levels of government. (Provinces received transfers from the federal government, while municipalities received transfers from both levels.)

In the case of provincial revenues, the figures for 1961 reflect the tax agreement that was in effect between the federal and provincial governments. Under the agreement the federal government "rented" the provinces' rights to tax personal incomes. In effect, the provinces relinquished their right to tax personal incomes in return for cash payments from the federal government which collected all the taxes.[4] Accordingly, the tax-collection statistics for 1961 do not reflect the division of the revenues produced but only which level of government actually collected them.

In 1991, the collection figures more closely matched the revenue divided between federal and provincial governments due to the fact that revenue-sharing agreements have been gradually modified to eliminate tax rental arrangements and shared-cost programs. In the years following 1978, the provinces have had, increasingly, to raise their own revenue. As a consequence, tax receipts by different levels of government will more closely reflect the actual sharing of tax revenues. To a considerable degree this evolution reflects the changing attitudes of the partners in Canadian confederation, and the changing tax arrangements are the harbinger of a more decentralized federation. (In the case of Quebec, separate tax collection facilities have been in existence for some time.)

The relationship between provincial and municipal government revenues reflects a different process. Municipalities now collect much

---

4   A documentation of these developments can be found in Lewis, "The Tangled Tale of Taxes and Transfers."

less of their total revenue in the form of taxes than they did in 1961. And, in fact, fully 49.7 percent of municipal revenue is now accounted for by transfers from federal and provincial governments—mainly the latter. In part, the emerging role of municipalities as dependencies of the provincial government is a result of decreasing reliance on property taxation as a form of finance (see Table 1.1). Property taxes accounted for only 10.0 percent of total taxes (of all kinds) in 1991 as opposed to 15.5 percent in 1961 (see Figure 1.2).

This trend toward less reliance on property taxation contrasts sharply with the situation in the United States and in California, in particular, where the sudden increase in property taxation touched off what has been called the "Proposition 13" movement. The failure of similar initiatives in Canada, the most recent in Toronto in 1991, may be

Table 1.4: Taxes collected by federal, provincial and municipal governments (billions of dollars)

	Federal		Provincial		Municipal	
	1991	1961	1991	1961	1991	1961
Personal Income Taxes	67.1	2.0	40.8	0.1	0.0	0.0
Corporate Income Taxes	11.0	0.3	5.2	1.0	0.0	0.0
General Sales Taxes	17.6	0.3	19.5	1.0	0.0	0.0
Property Tax	0.0	0.0	2.2	0.0	23.1	1.3
Health & Social Insurance Levies	15.3	5.0	9.9	0.2	0.0	0.0
Natural Resource Revenues	0.1	0.0	6.1	0.3	0.0	0.0
Customs Duties	4.1	0.5	0.0	0.0	0.0	0.0
Other Taxes	11.6	0.6	18.6	1.1	0.6	0.1
Total	126.8	4.8	102.4	2.9	23.8	1.4

Table 1.4: *continued*
(percent)

	Federal		Provincial		Municipal	
	1991	**1961**	**1991**	**1961**	**1991**	**1961**
Personal Income Taxes	62.2%	95.2%	37.8%	4.8%	0.0%	0.0%
Corporate Income Taxes	67.9	23.1	32.1	76.9	0.0	0.0
General Sales Taxes	47.4	23.1	52.5	76.9	0.1	0.0
Property Tax	0.0	0.0	8.8	0.0	91.2	100.0
Health & Social Insurance Levies	60.7	96.2	39.3	3.8	0.0	0.0
Natural Resource Revenues	1.2	0.0	98.8	100.0	0.0	0.0
Customs Duties	100.0	100.0	0.0	0.0	0.0	0.0
Other Taxes	37.5	33.3	60.4	61.1	2.0	5.6
Total	50.1	52.7	40.5	31.9	9.4	15.4

Source: See Table 1.1.

directly attributable to the different strategy of local government finance pursued in this country.

The fifth column

Hidden taxation

Most people are aware of the fact that they pay income tax, sales tax and property tax, the so-called direct taxes. Many others, appropriately, regard the various social security levies like Unemployment Insurance contributions and Canada and Quebec Pension Plan payments, as taxes. Similarly, many families know how much of these taxes they pay, either in terms of the rate (in the case of provincial sales taxes) or the total amount (in the case of property and income taxes). There are, however, many taxes of which Canadians, by and large, are unaware. These taxes are built into the price of goods and services but are not identified to the final consumer as a tax cost. For want of a better name, we call these implicit or hidden taxes.

Indirect taxes

There are several different kinds of hidden tax. Most well known of these are the so-called indirect taxes—principally excise taxes on such items as tobacco and alcohol, manufacturers' sales taxes, and import duties. These taxes are paid by some intermediary in the production process and become incorporated in the final price of the product. The most notorious examples are tobacco, liquor and gasoline taxes. (See Figures 1.3 and 1.4 for a breakdown of taxes paid for a litre of gasoline and a bottle of liquor.) In the case of liquor, the federal rate of indirect tax is 120 percent. In addition, alcohol bears a provincial government "mark-up" as well as a provincial sales tax. The final delivered price of alcohol is 429 percent above the price received by the distiller. The tax on tobacco is even more aggressive. The final consumer of both of these products pays the taxes without them having been identified as such. Of course, most people are aware that alcohol and tobacco are highly taxed, even if they do not know the actual rate of tax.

During 1991, total indirect taxes of all kinds amounted to 85.2 billion dollars in Canada. This was 12.5 percent of total Canadian income and accounted for 33.7 percent of total government revenue from taxation. In other words, quite apart from the tax they pay when they receive their incomes, Canadians pay, on average, a further 12.5 percent in indirect taxes when they spend their income. Furthermore, one-third of all government revenue is collected in this indirect-hidden form.

The hot potatoes—passing tax forward

Hidden taxes are hard to calculate because people try to pass them on to others. From the point of view of the individual, any tax that can be avoided is money in his or her pocket. As a result, people throughout the economy are constantly attempting to avoid situations in which they will have to pay taxes, and seeking to pay as little tax as possible,

Figure 1.3: Government take from a litre of gasoline

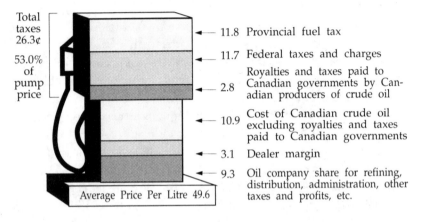

BRITISH COLUMBIA
Pump Price - Unleaded Gasoline

Total
taxes
26.3¢

53.0%
of
pump
price

◄─── 11.8 Provincial fuel tax

◄─── 11.7 Federal taxes and charges

◄─── 2.8 Royalties and taxes paid to Canadian governments by Canadian producers of crude oil

◄─── 10.9 Cost of Canadian crude oil excluding royalties and taxes paid to Canadian governments

◄─── 3.1 Dealer margin

◄─── 9.3 Oil company share for refining, distribution, administration, other taxes and profits, etc.

Average Price Per Litre 49.6

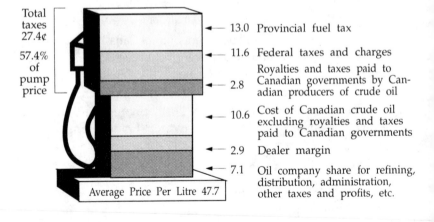

ONTARIO
Pump Price - Unleaded Gasoline

Total
taxes
27.4¢

57.4%
of
pump
price

◄─── 13.0 Provincial fuel tax

◄─── 11.6 Federal taxes and charges

◄─── 2.8 Royalties and taxes paid to Canadian governments by Canadian producers of crude oil

◄─── 10.6 Cost of Canadian crude oil excluding royalties and taxes paid to Canadian governments

◄─── 2.9 Dealer margin

◄─── 7.1 Oil company share for refining, distribution, administration, other taxes and profits, etc.

Average Price Per Litre 47.7

Figure 1.3: *Continued*

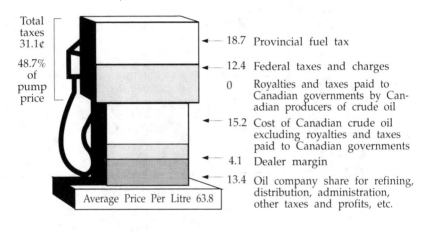

QUEBEC
Pump Price - Unleaded Gasoline

Total taxes 31.1¢

48.7% of pump price

← 18.7 Provincial fuel tax

← 12.4 Federal taxes and charges

0 Royalties and taxes paid to Canadian governments by Canadian producers of crude oil

← 15.2 Cost of Canadian crude oil excluding royalties and taxes paid to Canadian governments

← 4.1 Dealer margin

← 13.4 Oil company share for refining, distribution, administration, other taxes and profits, etc.

Average Price Per Litre 63.8

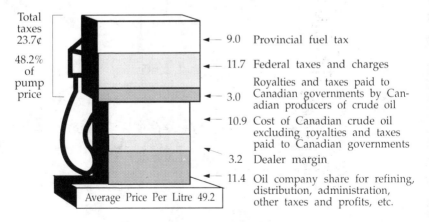

ALBERTA
Pump Price - Unleaded Gasoline

Total taxes 23.7¢

48.2% of pump price

← 9.0 Provincial fuel tax

← 11.7 Federal taxes and charges

← 3.0 Royalties and taxes paid to Canadian governments by Canadian producers of crude oil

← 10.9 Cost of Canadian crude oil excluding royalties and taxes paid to Canadian governments

3.2 Dealer margin

← 11.4 Oil company share for refining, distribution, administration, other taxes and profits, etc.

Average Price Per Litre 49.2

Source: *Where Does Your Gasoline Dollar Go?*, Petroleum Resources Communication Foundation.

Figure 1.4: Government take from a bottle of liquor

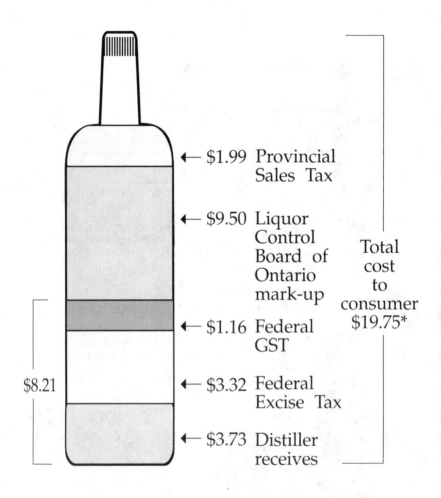

← $1.99 Provincial Sales Tax

← $9.50 Liquor Control Board of Ontario mark-up

Total cost to consumer $19.75*

← $1.16 Federal GST

← $3.32 Federal Excise Tax

$8.21

← $3.73 Distiller receives

Source: Association of Canadian Distillers, November, 1991.

* includes $0.05 freight.

Figure 1.5: Take home pay versus gross pay

In 1991 an employee in Ontario with $28,274 in taxable income had to receive an 8.5 percent pay increase to realize a 5 percent increase in after-tax pay. Tax rates vary by province and comparable figures for the other provinces are presented in the table below.

Percent wage increase required for a 5 percent increase in after-tax income
(assessed income at $28,274)

Nfld	PEI	NS	NB	Que	Ont	Man	Sask	Alta	BC
8.8	8.7	8.7	8.8	9.3	8.5	8.7	8.7	8.3	8.4

Source: Canadian Tax Foundation, *The National Finances*, 1991.

whatever their situation. The moonlighting tradesman who engages in "cash only" transactions; the mechanic who fixes his neighbour's truck in return for free cartage; the dentists who fix fellow dentists' families' teeth on a reciprocal basis; the tycoon whose business is "incorporated" in the Grand Cayman Islands: all want to avoid taxes. In the end though, somebody ends up paying. Who that somebody is, is one of the most difficult and important questions in economics and is known as the study of "tax incidence."

How employees pass the tax on

To get an idea of the difficulties involved, consider the following: The average Canadian employee measures his welfare in terms of after-tax dollars, and in each new wage bargain aims to get an increase in take-home pay. The fact that an increase in gross terms will imply a smaller increase in after-tax dollars motivates the employee or his union representative to demand a larger gross increase. By doing so, the employee is attempting to get the employer to bear the burden of the additional tax. For an example of this process see the box insert—Figure 1.5.

Expressed slightly differently, the employee who bargains in this manner is attempting to "pass the tax forward." His behaviour is not unique but, on the contrary, is a general characteristic of all employees in the Canadian economy. Corporations attempt to pass their higher profits and payroll taxes forward to the consumer in the form of higher prices (as well as backward on employees in the form of lower wages). Of course, all of these attempts may or may not be successful in any single instance, and they will be accomplished to varying degrees through time.

Who pays the indirect taxes?

It is difficult to know where the burden of these taxes ultimately lies, but not impossible. We simply need to make intelligent assumptions about how each tax is passed on. For example, a general sales tax is collected and remitted to government by retailers. It is clear, however, that in most cases the retailers do not actually bear the tax—they are merely the agents for collecting it. The actual effect of the tax is to increase the price of all goods and services affected by the tax and to cause a corresponding reduction in the purchasing power of family incomes. Accordingly, to the extent that a general sales tax causes an increase in the general level of prices, the tax is borne not by the collectors but by income earners in the economy whose incomes now buy less. Indirect or sales taxes therefore burden all income earned in the economy.

Payroll taxes such as unemployment insurance premiums and Canada and Quebec Pension Plan contributions are collected in part from the employer and in part from the employee. And, while no one would dispute the fact that the employee pays the employee portion, in most cases it is true that the employee will also pay the so-called employer's portion. This is because the payroll tax paid by the employer reduces the total amount of money the employer has available to pay labour-related costs. In other words, payroll taxes reduce potential wage and salary payments below what they would otherwise have been. Since no corresponding reduction can be expected in the price of the products that the employee will want to purchase, the payroll tax, in effect, burdens the employee.

While both of these arguments have been framed in terms of employees and their wages and salaries, it is clear that taxes burden capital income as well. For example, a general sales tax reduces the purchasing power of all income, not just wage and salary income. As a result, it is appropriate to view the general sales tax burden as falling on all forms of income, including interest income and dividends. All of the tax burden estimates constructed in this study therefore allocate the burden of general sales taxes in proportion to all income received by a family. In practical terms, this means that if general sales taxes amount to 6 percent of total Canadian income in a particular year, we would add 6 percent of a family's total income to the family's tax bill when we calculate how much tax the family pays.

In computing this general sales tax burden, income that a family receives from government is explicitly ignored. The reason for this is that the payments received from government, such as the Old Age Pension and Family Allowance, have historically been and are currently either directly or indirectly indexed to the general level of prices (that is, increased to offset the effects of inflation). As the general price level rises in step with the sales tax, the purchasing power of transfers from government is not permitted to fall. As a consequence, the general sales tax does not have the effect of burdening income in this form, and it would be inappropriate to allocate any part of the burden of general sales taxes to this sort of income.[5]

While the burden of a general sales tax and payroll taxes is relatively straightforward to assign, the assignment of particular excise taxes is a little more elusive. Whereas a general sales tax increases all prices and hence reduces the purchasing power of all incomes, particular taxes on commodities usually affect only the price of that commodity. For example, excise taxes imposed on liquor, motor vehicles, and fuels affect only the prices of those products, in the first instance at least. (Ultimately, of course, they may affect a whole range of prices—fuel taxes affect the

---

5   This particular distinction is due to the work of Edgar K. Browning and William R. Johnson of the University of Virginia who have completed a study of the burden of taxation in the United States: *The Distribution of the Tax Burden,* American Enterprise Institute, 1979.

price of transportation, as do motor vehicle taxes. These taxes may therefore have an overall effect although levied only on a particular product.)

In light of these considerations, it has been the usual practice when calculating tax burdens to allocate the burden of particular excise taxes according to the consumption of those items. The 1976 tax burden studies published by The Fraser Institute employed this methodology.[6] However, following this methodology gives rise to a variety of problems. First of all, only the first round effects of the excise tax are incorporated and, hence, the actual distribution of the tax burden may differ substantially from the estimate. Secondly, this method may not even provide good estimates of the first round effects of the tax. This is so because the relative burden of a particular tax borne by a family is determined not by the family's consumption of the taxed item but by the fraction of the family's income spent on the item relative to the national average.[7]

In view of these problems with the traditional approach, and given that the proportions of income spent on different items by various income groups do not vary widely from the average, we decided for the purposes of this study to distribute excise taxes in the same way as general sales taxes. That is to say, it is assumed that excise taxes burden total incomes—excluding government transfers to persons.

So, the answer to the question, "Who pays the indirect taxes?" is a straightforward one. Although indirect taxes appear in a variety of forms, they ultimately burden the income that the family earns.

Other taxes by other names

In addition to "formal" taxes levied by government, there are a variety of other government actions which, while having the same effect as

---

6   These studies, published in 1976 and 1977, respectively, were: *How Much Tax Do You Really Pay?*, M. Walker (editor), and *Income and Taxation in Canada 1961-1975*, S.C. Pipes and S. Star, The Fraser Institute.

7   Edgar K. Browning and William R. Johnson, *The Distribution of the Tax Burden*, American Enterprise Institute, 1979.

taxes, are not normally identified as such. These activities are becoming an increasingly important feature of the Canadian economic landscape and must receive special mention.

Clothing and textile taxes

In November 1976, the federal government imposed a quota on imported clothing and textiles. Its purpose was to limit the importation of inexpensive clothing and textiles and so protect Canadian markets for Canadian clothing and textile manufacturers. The associated decline in competition for the Canadian consumer's clothing expenditure dollar will undoubtedly have produced a higher price for clothing than would otherwise have existed (particularly since world-wide clothing and textile markets are in a depressed state owing to expanded output from Far Eastern producers).

The difference between the price for clothing that would have prevailed in the absence of the quota and the price that actually prevails is a tax on the consumer. Proceeds from this tax go directly to producers and are, in effect, a producer subsidy. There is no difference in principle between this sort of tax and the other hidden taxes that we have been discussing. Of course, these "clothing taxes" do not show up in government revenue figures, and precise estimates of their size are difficult to make, but we cannot ignore their existence. In their book, *Free Trade Between the United States and Canada*, R. J. and P. Wonnacott have estimated that the total amount of tax levied in the form of tariff protection or other barriers to international competition may be as high as 10.5 percent of Canada's Gross National Product.[8] Currently, this amounts to a tax of over 71 billion dollars.

Some of the burden associated with tariffs and quotas will be eliminated as a result of the Free Trade Agreement between Canada and the United States. However, in many cases the principal source of cheaper products is not the United States but other, and in particular Third World countries.

---

8   R. J. Wonnacott and P. Wonnacott, *Free Trade Between the United States and Canada*, Cambridge, Mass.: Harvard University Press, 1967, p. 299.

Marketing board taxes

At present, there are some 177 farm products' cartels in Canada. These cartels or marketing boards generally have the effect of suppressing competition in the production of the cartelized product, and they consequently cause the price of the product to be higher than it otherwise would have been. As in the case of clothing and textiles, the amount by which the marketing board price exceeds the price that would prevail in its absence—that is, in the market—is a tax on the consumer. Accordingly, marketing boards ought to be viewed as a device for transferring money from consumers to producers. And this transfer is equivalent to a tax on consumers, the proceeds of which are given to producers.

The increasing power of marketing boards, and the seeming reluctance of government to restrain their growth (the federal Minister of Agriculture actually fosters their growth), suggests that these marketing board taxes will become increasingly important in Canada. Moreover, as restraint in government taxation and spending becomes a reality, it will become increasingly expedient for government to rely on hidden "regulatory" taxation of this sort. Fortunately offsetting this tendency is the pressure which free trade will exert on the political groups which support these developments.

Regulatory taxation

In general, a government can achieve a given objective either by taxation and subsidization or by regulation—rather than imposing import quotas, the federal government could have assisted Canadian clothing manufacturers by giving them a direct subsidy financed from general tax revenue. That the government chooses to use regulation to convey a subsidy in this fashion should not distract attention from the fact that a subsidy has been provided, and that it is the Canadian consumer who pays for it.

A study by Moroz and Brown (1987) tried to measure the costs of some of the hidden taxes mentioned above. They estimated the dollar value of protection to Canadian industries in 1979 due to tariffs and non-tariff barriers such as import quotas. The sum of such protection across industries was $32.2 billion in 1991 dollars, or 10.4 percent of the total value of production. Most of the protection went to textiles, agriculture, and forestry. In sum, each Canadian paid $1,355 in hidden taxes on internationally-traded items in 1979. More up-to-date figures on agricultural protection (OECD, 1992) suggest that farmers received $8.8 billion in protection in 1991.

Deferred taxation

During his budget statement in November 1978, Mr. Jean Chretien, then Federal Minister of Finance, made much of the fact that because the personal income tax structure had been indexed to inflation, there had, in effect, been a reduction in personal income taxation compared to what would have prevailed in the absence of indexing. That is to say, exemptions had been increased by the rate of inflation and tax brackets had been shifted to ensure that incomes swollen by inflation would not be taxed more heavily on that account alone. While this change in the tax structure, first introduced in 1974, was indeed a welcome one, it would be naïve to uncritically accept the move as a permanent reduction in the government's propensity to tax.

In fact, the "reduction" in personal income tax revenues was accompanied—starting in 1975—by deficits and shortfalls in the federal government's cash position which were unprecedented in peacetime.

Although this situation is not entirely attributable to the decline in personal income tax revenues, it is clearly the case that continued growth in income taxation could have meant a smaller deficit and a reduction in net cash requirements to be financed by issuing debt. Accordingly, in assessing Canada's current level of taxation, it is appropriate to take into account the extent to which tax collections are merely deferred by current tax "reductions."

In other words, when calculating the total tax burden of all government operations in a given year, it is appropriate to include not only current taxes levied but also future taxes which must be levied to discharge debts acquired by the government in the current year. To the extent that government finances its operations by deficit financing or issuing bonds—deferred taxation—there is a hidden tax burden implicit in its operations. In Chapter 4 we have calculated estimates of the total tax burden which include all of these deferred taxes.

How much tax should Canadians pay?

In 1917 when he first introduced the Personal Income Tax, the Finance Minister of the day, Sir Thomas White, was of the opinion that no Canadians should pay tax on income less than $2,000 if they were single and had no dependents. Married taxpayers, he said, should pay tax on income in excess of $3,000. The tax structure that ultimately evolved provided that single Canadians pay income tax on income in excess of $1,500, while married Canadians were exempted from the tax until their incomes exceeded $3,000. However, in the very next year, this was reduced to $2,000 for a married taxpayer and $1,000 for single Canadians.[9]

While the tax structure has gone through many changes in the intervening years, it is interesting to ask how Canadians would be treated for tax purposes in 1991-92 if this initial view of "ability to pay" had kept pace with developments in people's incomes. To answer this question we have adjusted the original exemption levels by the increase in average wages over the period since 1917. This adjustment yields an exemption level for 1991 of $10,694 for single taxpayers and $21,387 for married taxpayers. But actual personal credits for single and married taxpayers amounted to $6,280 and $11,513 in 1991—in each case less than the level that would have been allowed if the 1917 standard had continued in force.

The reason for the disparity is that over the years from 1917 to 1974 exemption levels were not indexed to the cost of living or the increase in family incomes—in fact, in a few years during the depression, exemption levels were actually reduced. Since 1974, exemption levels have been indexed to the rate of inflation.

---

9   House of Commons Debates, July 25, 1917, p. 3,765.

Chapter 2

Personal Income Taxation in Canada

IN CHAPTER 1 WE ALLUDED to the fact that income taxes are the largest single source of government revenue. It therefore follows that the largest single tax paid by the average Canadian family is the income tax. As we also noted in Chapter 1, this tax came into existence in 1917 as a "temporary" emergency measure to help finance the increasing debt associated with World War I. "Nothing," it is said, "endures like the temporary."

The current income tax structure

Table 2.1 presents the actual rates of income tax (both federal and provincial) encountered by the average single individual at various taxable income levels, for 1990 and 1991. As the figures show, the minimum rate of tax is 26.69 percent payable on taxable income of $1.00. The second rate is 40.82 percent payable on taxable income of $28,785 to $57,567 and the third and maximum rate is payable at income levels of $57,568 or higher and amounts to 46.98 percent of every dollar earned beyond that income level. These rates are the marginal rates of tax that a person encounters as he or she moves from one level of taxable income to the next. An equally interesting series of calculations relates to the amount of tax an individual theoretically pays on a given amount of total income (not taxable income). These rates are shown in Table 2.2.

Table 2.1: 1990 and 1991 combined federal and provincial personal income tax—marginal rates*

Taxable Income 1990		Taxable Income 1991	
$	%	$	%
1	26.69	1	26.69
28,276	40.82	28,785	40.82
56,551	46.40	57,568	46.98

Source: Canadian Tax Foundation, *The National Finances*, 1991, table 7.4.

*Tax rate which comes into effect with each additional amount of income.

In the case of a family, the situation can be slightly different because of credits permitted for the dependent spouse. Support of children also eases somewhat the tax burden on the taxpayer. In perusing tax rates for the average family of four presented in Table 2.3, the reader should bear in mind that this schedule of rates is not directly applicable for many families. In many cases, both adult members of the family declare taxable income. In this case they each file a separate return, and tax rates for individuals apply. Of course, this is to the advantage of the taxpayers. If, for example, a childless couple who are both working have the same income—say $15,000 per year—they pay total tax of about $3,924 (see table 2.4) when they file as individuals. If their total income of $30,000 were earned by only one of them, their total tax payable would be about $4,692—a difference of $768.

In other words, if their income is earned by one family member, the family pays a gross tax rate of 15.64 percent, but if their income is composed of two salaries the tax rate is only 13.08 percent. The difference between the two tax rates rises as the family income increases until very high income levels are reached (see Table 2.4). This difference between the single and double income-earner family will continue to affect the calculations in the remainder of this book. In particular, income tax payments shown in the various composite tax tables in Chapter 3 reflect the fact that, on average, tax payments are made by a mixture of single and double taxpayer families.

Table 2.2: Personal income tax paid (single taxpayer—no dependants) at selected levels of income, 1991

Total Income	Federal & Provincial Tax Rate	
Assessed ($)	Total Tax Payable ($)	Average (%)
7,500	57	0.8
10,000	692	6.9
12,500	1,327	10.6
15,000	1,962	13.1
17,500	2,597	14.8
20,000	3,232	16.2
25,000	4,512	18.0
30,000	6,134	20.4
50,000	14,259	28.5
100,000	37,210	37.2
200,000	84,190	42.1

Source: Canadian Tax Foundation, *The National Finances*, 1991, table 7.11.

Who pays the income tax bill?

While it is possible to calculate tax rates and amounts of tax payable on an "up-to-date" basis, analysis of the income tax system as a whole has to be based on two-year-old statistics. This arises because our conclusions about how much tax the average Canadian family pays is based in part on surveys of taxpayers which Statistics Canada conducts and releases with a two-year lag. Accordingly, our analysis of who pays the income tax—and of other related questions—must be based on 1989 data. For the most part, however, we can rest assured that the relative magnitudes involved will be stable over time and, hence, that conclusions reached are reliable for 1992.

Table 2.3: Personal income tax paid (married taxpayer— two dependant children under 16 years of age) at selected levels of income, 1991

Total Income	Federal & Provincial Tax Rate	
Assessed	Total Tax Payable ($)	Average (%)
17,500	$ (360)	–2.1%
20,000	275	1.4
25,000	1,626	6.5
30,000	3,683	12.3
50,000	12,977	26.0
100,000	33,359	33.4
200,000	83,339	41.7

Source: Canadian Tax Foundation, *The National Finances*, 1991, table 7.12.

In 1989, a total of $77.7 billion was paid by individuals in income taxes and, as Table 2.5 shows, nearly half of it was paid by individuals with incomes below $45,000. Individuals with incomes below $50,000 paid nearly 56 percent of the total income tax bill. In fact, 41 percent of all income taxes were paid by individuals with incomes in the relatively narrow range, $20,000 to $45,000.

Table 2.4: Tax rates and number of income earners, 1991

Total family income	One income earner		Two income earners	
	tax ($)	tax rate (%)	tax ($)	tax rate (%)
15,000	$ 565	3.76%	$ 114	0.76%
20,000	1,835	9.17	1,384	6.92
25,000	3,115	12.46	2,654	10.62
30,000	4,692	15.64	3,924	13.08
50,000	10,005	20.01	9,024	18.05
100,000	35,768	35.77	28,518	28.52
200,000	82,748	41.37	74,420	37.21

Source: Canadian Tax Foundation, *The National Finances*, 1991, chapter 7, and calculations by the authors.

As column 4 of Table 2.5 shows, over half of all taxable returns were filed by individuals with incomes less than $20,000. This proportion reflects the large number of part-time workers, students employed during the summer, and other intermittent workers earning low incomes. These taxpayers generated only 8.4 percent of total tax revenue, while the top 20.8 percent of taxpayers—those declaring income of $35,000 or more—contributed 68.1 percent of the total income tax bill.

An interesting aspect of the information in Table 2.5 is the relationship between taxes paid and income declared. For example, as noted above, 31.9 percent of the total income tax bill was paid by individuals with incomes below $35,000. From column 6 we discover that this group of individuals earned 48.3 percent of all the income declared. So, income earners below $35,000 paid a smaller proportion of the total tax bill than their share of total earned income might suggest. On the other hand, the top 20.8 percent of taxpayers, who had incomes in excess of $35,000, paid about 68.1 percent of the total tax bill while receiving only 51.7 percent of total income earned.

Table 2.5: An analysis of income, taxes, and tax returns by income class, 1989

Total income assessed	Percent-age of total tax paid by income class	Percent-age of total tax paid by all classes at or below this class level	Percent-age of total returns filed by this income class	Percent-age of total returns filed by all classes at or below this class level	Percent-age of total income de-clared by this income class	Percent-age of total income de-clared by all classes at or below this class level
Less than $5,000	0.01%	0.01%	16.39%	16.36%	1.20%	1.20%
$5,000-9,999	0.53	0.54	14.28	30.67	4.47	5.67
$10,000-14,999	2.74	3.28	12.59	43.25	6.56	12.23
$15,000-19,999	5.10	8.39	11.00	54.26	8.06	20.30
$20,000-24,999	6.94	15.33	9.77	64.03	9.21	29.50
$25,000-29,999	8.03	23.36	8.37	72.40	9.63	39.14
$30,000-34,999	8.58	31.95	6.77	79.17	9.20	48.34
$35,000-39,999	8.86	40.80	5.41	84.57	8.49	56.83
$40,000-44,999	8.26	49.06	4.09	88.67	7.29	64.11
$45,000-49,999	7.25	56.31	3.05	91.72	6.07	70.18
$50,000-99,999	24.79	81.10	7.05	98.77	18.75	88.94
$100,000-199,999	7.83	88.93	0.92	99.69	5.14	94.08
$200,000+	11.07	100.00	0.31	100.00	5.92	100.00

Source: 1991 Taxation Statistics, 1989 taxation year, Revenue Canada Taxation, Ottawa, 1991.

The reason for this, of course, is the fact that the income tax structure is "progressive." That is, it takes a larger fraction from high incomes than it does from low incomes, as is clear from the tax rates presented in Table 2.4. Sales taxes also contribute to progressivity because even though they hit everyone at the same rate, there are sales tax rebates which vary inversely with income. Furthermore, many income transfers from the state are indexed to the price of goods, so that as the price rises due to a sales tax, so do the transfers. This eases the burden of sales taxes to the poor. We will come back to this point in the next chapter where we bring sales taxes more fully into the picture.

Get it from the rich

It is often said, and more often believed, that the key to "social welfare" or "social justice" is the redistribution of income. That is, take income from those who have much and give it to those who have little. The extreme form of this prescription is the formula "from each according to his ability [to pay?] and to each according to his need"—the rule advanced in the Communist Manifesto.[10]

Our analysis in the preceding section of who pays the income tax reveals that Canada as a country already engages in significant taxation of those who are relatively well-off. However, at least one prominent Canadian economist has suggested that Canada has not been successful in redistributing income from the rich to the poor—that ours is not a "Robin Hood" society.[11] It, therefore, remains interesting to ask whether or not we could achieve a more equal distribution of the benefits of the Canadian good life by taxing more of the income of the richest Canadians.

---

10   K. Marx and Friedrich Engels, *Manifesto of the Communist Party*, 1848.

11   W.I. Gillespie, *In Search of Robin Hood*, C.D. Howe Research Institute, Montreal, 1978.

How rich is rich?

The question that immediately arises is "How rich is rich?" At what level of income should the government tax away all increases in the interest of "equitable" income distribution? In view of the fact that members of Parliament earn in excess of $60,000 per year, it is unlikely that "Canadians" would find it equitable to confiscate earnings less than that level. Let us, then, for the sake of illustration, select $60,000 as the maximum income that Canadians should be allowed to earn. Under this rule, all incomes above that level would be subject to a 100 percent rate of income tax, and the proceeds would be distributed to all income earners with incomes less than $60,000.

Counting the rich

In 1989, 884,150 persons filed tax returns reporting income of $60,000 or more. Total income reported by these people was $93.0 billion. If the government had really taxed away all income beyond $59,999, total tax revenue in 1989 would have been $16.5 billion higher than it actually was. Redistribution of this increased tax revenue to those (17 million people) with incomes less than $60,000 would yield an average annual payment of $945.00 for each person submitting a tax return.

Taxing the "rich," not the source of wealth

This calculation is an important one because it reveals the practical impossibility of "getting it from the rich and redistributing it to the poor." Those who are impatient with the speed at which the economic process improves the condition of the poorest members of society ought to reflect on the fact that the same (or larger) total increase in the incomes of those earning less than $60,000 would be achieved by about 4.9 percent growth in total incomes even if it were distributed in exactly the same way as it is currently.

Chapter 3

How Much Tax Do You Really Pay?

THE ISSUES DISCUSSED IN CHAPTER 2 focus on the income tax bill that Canadians pay. But income tax represents less than half of the total taxes paid by the average Canadian family. The purpose of this chapter is to expand the analysis of taxation to include all taxes that Canadians pay.

How much income do you really earn?

Cash income

In order to properly calculate how much tax a person (or a group) pays, it is necessary first to determine their income. While this process may seem simple, what a person's income seems to be is very different from what it actually is. This section of the chapter, therefore, explains the method for deriving the income figures used in subsequent sections.

The ultimate goal of income calculations is to determine the total income a Canadian citizen would have if there were no taxes of any sort and other factors remained unchanged. To arrive at such a figure, it is necessary to discover all the income sources a person might have and all of the taxes that might have been paid on this income before the person received it, and finally to add up all of the income taxes.

The first layer of income items is easily discovered: wages, salaries, interest from savings bonds, rent from the in-law suite in the basement, or even rent on "the back forty." These sorts of items comprise what in this study is called cash income.

Cash income and underreporting

In its regular surveys of household income, Statistics Canada finds that people typically omit some income items when they estimate their cash income—that is, they underreport their income. The particular items omitted vary from family to family, but, on average, families tend to underestimate their total income by 4 to 12 percent. Items that might be omitted include miscellaneous interest income, income from "moonlighting," and so on. Fortunately, Statistics Canada does have a comprehensive measure of income in the National Accounts framework, and it is therefore possible not only to know that the survey information is incorrect but also to adjust that information to make it more accurate.[12] Accordingly, cash income estimates used in this study have been adjusted to make them consistent with the comprehensive income figures contained in the National Accounts.

It may be useful at this stage to provide an example based on a fictitious individual. In order to make the example as comprehensive as possible, it is assumed that the individual involved in the example has income from all of the sources identified in the study—an unlikely circumstance for any real individual. The example is presented in Table 3.1.

---

12   Statistics Canada, System of National Accounts, *National Income and Expenditure Accounts*, catalogue no. 13-201, Supply and Services Canada.

Table 3.1: Cash income, 1992

Wages & Salaries	$ 39,716
Income From Farm Operations	390
Unincorporated Non-farm Income	1,892
Interest	3,285
Dividends	502
Private Pension Payments	2,067
Government Pension Payments	483
Family Allowance*	387
Old Age Pension Payments	1,088
Other Transfers From Government	3,724
Equals Cash Income	$53,535

Source: Fraser Institute Canadian Tax Simulator (CANTASIM).

*Income from government is commonly refered to as a negative tax or a transfer payment.

Total income

In addition to cash income most families also have various forms of non-cash income that must be included in a comprehensive income figure. For example, most wage and salary earners receive fringe benefits as a condition of their employment. Also part of an employee's income is the investment income accumulated by his or her pension plan and the interest accumulated—though not paid—on his or her insurance policy.

At a higher level of subtlety, a comprehensive income total should also include a number of other income sources. For example, a homeowner is, in effect, his or her own landlord. Therefore, the homeowner receives rental income. Because this implicit income is not paid in cash, its existence must be "imputed" or assigned to the homeowner.

The reason for including such income in a comprehensive income measure is that the homeowner could actually earn that income by renting the premises to somebody else. On the same basis, income is imputed for the rental of farm properties. Income is also imputed on account of interest-free loans that people make. The interest foregone is in fact implicit income in the form of a gift.

Profits not paid out as dividends by corporations but held in the form of retained earnings are, in fact, income of the shareholders of the corporation, even though they do not receive it in the year in which it is reported. Also, bad debts which are written off by corporations are, in fact, a source of net income to the debtor and are treated as such. Finally, food consumed by farm operators is evaluated at market price and attributed to farm operators as income.

Again to make the calculation clear, the total income figure is accumulated in Table 3.2 for a fictitious individual who is assumed to have income from all sources.

Table 3.2: Total income, 1992

Cash Income	$53,535
Plus Fringe Benefits from Employment	4,514
Investment Income of Insurance Companies	1,107
Investment Income of Trusteed Pension Plans	1,599
Imputed Interest	399
Value of Food from Farms	17
Corporate Retained Earnings	511
Bad Debts	82
Equals Total Income	$61,764

Source: Fraser Institute Canadian Tax Simulator (CANTASIM).

Table 3.3: Total income before tax, 1992

Wages & Salaries	$39,716
Income from Farm Operations	390
Unincorporated Non-farm Income	1,892
Interest	3,285
Dividends	502
Private Pension Payments	2,067
Government Pension Payments	483
Family Allowance	387
Old Age Pension Payments	1,088
Other Transfers from Government	3,724
Equals Cash Income	53,535
Plus Fringe Benefits from Employment	4,514
Investment Income of Insurance Companies	1,107
Investment Income of Trusteed Pension Plans	1,599
Imputed Interest	399
Value of Food from Farms	17
Corporate Retained Earnings	511
Bad Debts	82
Equals Total Income	61,764
Plus Property Taxes	1,748
Profit Taxes	1,267
Indirect Taxes	9,944
Equals Total Income Before Tax	$74,723

Source: Fraser Institute Canadian Tax Simulator (CANTASIM).

Total income before tax

Some of the income earned by Canadians is taxed before they receive it. For example, shareholders receive dividends on corporate profits after corporate profit taxes have been paid. In the absence of taxes, the dividends (or retained earnings) of the shareholder would have been higher. Therefore, in order to arrive at a total income before tax, it is necessary to add back the corporate profits collected from corporations. Similarly, if there were no property taxes, net after-tax rental income would be higher than it actually is. Therefore, before-tax income must be augmented by the amount of property taxes paid.

In the discussion of indirect and hidden taxes in Chapter 1, it was noted that these taxes reduce the effective income available to Canadians because they increase the price of items that people buy with their incomes. In effect, income after tax is less, in terms of the things it will buy, than it was before tax. In order to arrive at an estimate of before-tax income it is necessary, therefore, to add back to incomes the reduction brought about by indirect taxes.

Finally, payroll taxes levied on firms are, as noted earlier, effectively paid by employees, because the taxes reduce the amount of money available to pay wages and salaries. Accordingly, it is necessary to add back the amount of payroll taxes to employees' incomes to arrive at a before-tax total income estimate.

Table 3.3 presents an example of a complete income calculation for a fictitious individual who is assumed to have income from all of the income sources identified in the study and to have paid all of the identified taxes.

Calculating the total tax bill

Basically, the tax calculation for the average Canadian family consists of adding up the various taxes that the family pays. Hidden taxes such as taxes on tobacco and alcohol are allocated according to the method indicated in Chapter 1. To preserve consistency, the family used, by way of example, in the tax calculation in Table 3.4 is the same family used in the income calculation.

Table 3.4: Tax bill of the average Canadian family, 1992

Cash Income	$53,535
Total Income Before Tax	74,723

Taxes

Income Taxes	9,106
Profit Taxes	1,267
Sales Taxes	3,748
Liquor, Tobacco, Amusement, and Other Excise Taxes	1,180
Auto, Fuel, & Motor Vehicle Licence Taxes	738
Social Security, Medical & Hospital Taxes	4,171
Property Taxes	1,748
Natural Resource Taxes	259
Import Duties	533
Other Taxes	787
Total Taxes	$23,537

Taxes as a Percentage of

Cash Income	44%
Total Income Before Tax	31%

Source: Fraser Institute Canadian Tax Simulator (CANTASIM).

Chapter 4

The Canadian Consumer Tax Index

Introduction

A S NOTED IN PRECEDING CHAPTERS, Canada's system of taxation is enormously complex. This complexity makes it extremely difficult to describe the tax system in a simple way—difficult to provide a few concise numbers or words to characterize it at any given time. Any discussion of the tax system—even a simplified one—is likely to be complicated because the system has so many different aspects. As we showed in Chapter 1, even counting the number of taxes is a difficult business. Also complicated is the pattern of tax rates—who pays what—and, of course, the changes in these factors over a period of time. In fact, this book attempts to provide a simplified description of how the tax system is evolving—and, natural pride of authorship notwithstanding, this is not a simple book.

Why construct a Consumer Tax Index?

For individual taxpayers, the most interesting variable for Canadians is how much tax they actually have to pay. In 1976, when we wrote the Fraser Institute's first tax study, *How Much Tax Do You Really Pay?*, we devised an index which we called the Consumer Tax Index. Its purpose was to provide a summary-at-a-glance indicator of what has been happening to the tax bill faced by the average Canadian family over the years since 1961.

Some readers of that book found the tax index too simple—it failed to take into account how the tax money was spent by governments and, therefore, showed only one side of the ledger.[13] On the other hand, the index in that first study and in all subsequent studies has been widely used by financial and consumer affairs columnists across the country to describe how the Canadian tax system has evolved. Moreover, it has been in continuous use ever since its release and has been described as the most up-to-date measure of the extent of Canadian taxation. It was particularly widely cited during the summer of 1978 in the wake of the California tax revolt—the so-called "Proposition 13" movement.

During 1988 Statistics Canada approached the Institute to enquire about how the Consumer Tax Index is calculated. That interest was motivated by the advent in Canada of the broadly applied Goods and Services Tax and the desire, on the part of the agency, to provide a measure of the impact which the new tax would have on the rate of inflation. In 1990, Statistics Canada indicated that it would not proceed because of methodological problems that would be associated with such a measurement. In view of the high political interest which would attach to such a number, one can appreciate their reluctance.

In any event, The Fraser Institute's Consumer Tax Index remains, therefore, the only readily available comprehensive index of direct and indirect taxation available.

While it is easy to acknowledge that any single measure of something as complex as the Canadian tax system is bound to be incomplete,

---

13   Don McGillivray, "An Over-Simplified Look At Our Complicated Taxes," *Financial Times of Canada*, November 8, 1976.

it is our view that the Canadian Consumer Tax Index is a useful and important indicator of a very important economic magnitude. As noted, it remains the only widely available measurement of its kind. In this spirit we shall continue to calculate and publish the Consumer Tax Index and other associated statistics, in our ongoing assessment of the Canadian tax system.

What is the Canadian Consumer Tax Index?

The Consumer Tax Index is an index of the total dollar tax bill paid by the average Canadian family. It is constructed by calculating the tax bill of an average Canadian family for each of the years included in the index. The index below, therefore, shows the tax bill for a family with an income of $5,000 in 1961, for a family with an income of $8,000 in 1969, and so on. Now, while each of these families was average, in an income sense, in each year selected, it is not necessarily the same family. The objective is not to trace the tax experience of a particular family but rather to plot the experience of a family which was average in each year.

The index thus answers the question, "How has the tax burden of the average family changed since 1961, bearing in mind the fact that the average family has changed in that period?" To be clear about some of the questions the index will not answer, we can note that the average family in 1992 is headed by a younger person, who is more likely to own a car, less likely to own a house, and has fewer members than the average family in 1961. Most important, the family's earned income increased by 971 percent over the period.

The basis of the tax index is the total tax calculation presented in Table 4.1. Income and tax calculations were made for a selection of years beginning in 1961 and culminating in 1992. The tax bill of the average family yielded by this process was then converted to index form. The results are reported in Table 4.2 and Figure 4.1. They show that the tax bill of the average Canadian family has increased by 1305.2 percent over the period since 1961, and that the index has a value of 1405.2 in 1992.

At least part of that increase reflects the effects of inflation. In order to eliminate the effect of the declining value of the dollar, we have also calculated the tax index in real dollars—that is, dollars of 1981 purchasing power. While this adjustment has the effect of reducing the steepness of the index's path over time, the real-dollar tax index, nevertheless, increased by 162.8 percent over the period (see Table 4.3).

What the Consumer Tax Index shows

The dramatic increase in the Consumer Tax Index over the period 1961-1992 was produced by the interaction of a number of factors. First, there was a dramatic increase in incomes over the period, and even with

Table 4.1: Taxes paid by the average Canadian family, 1961-1992

Year	Average Cash Income ($)	Total Income Before Tax ($)	Taxes Paid ($)	Increase in Taxes Paid over Base Year (%)
1961	5,000	7,582	1,675	—
1969	8,000	11,323	3,117	86.1
1972	10,000	14,154	4,203	150.9
1974	12,500	17,976	5,429	224.1
1976	16,500	21,872	5,979	257.0
1978	18,500	27,627	8,343	398.1
1981	26,000	39,236	12,475	644.8
1984	34,216	48,866	17,129	922.6
1986	38,376	55,356	15,141	803.9
1987	41,156	60,599	19,519	1065.3
1988	44,192	65,248	21,069	1157.9
1989	47,987	67,358	21,142	1162.2
1990	50,319	69,788	22,284	1230.4
1991	51,092	71,011	22,486	1242.4
1992	53,535	74,723	23,537	1305.2

Source: Fraser Institute Canadian Tax Simulator (CANTASIM).

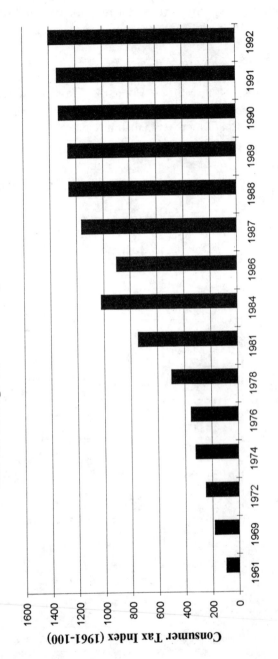

Figure 4.1
The Canadian Consumer Tax Index, 1961-1992:
How the Average Canadian Family's Tax Burden has Grown

no change in tax rates, the family's tax bill would have increased substantially. In the absence of a change in the tax rate, growth in family income alone would have produced an increase in the tax bill from $1,675 in 1961 to $17,934 in 1992. The second contributing factor was a 31 percent increase in the tax rate faced by the average family.

Table 4.2: Consumer Tax Index
1961=100

Year	
1961	100.0
1969	186.1
1972	250.9
1974	324.1
1976	357.0
1978	498.1
1981	744.8
1984	1022.6
1986	903.9
1987	1165.3
1988	1257.9
1989	1262.2
1990	1330.4
1991	1342.4
1992	1405.2

Source: Table 4.1.

From the mid 1970s to the late 1980s, the rate of increase in the tax bill slowed appreciably, reflecting a decline in the overall rate of taxation and an increase in the extent to which all governments resorted to issuing debt—that is, bonds—to finance their expenditures. The early 1990s have seen a shift back to taxation as Ottawa and the provinces have begun to recognize the need to pay the debt. Instead of lowering spending to pay for the debt, most governments have chosen to rely chiefly on raising taxes.

Introducing deficits into the individual's tax picture gives us a better idea of this hidden burden of government. The size of this burden shows up most clearly in a comparison of the Consumer Tax Index and the Fraser Institute's Balanced Budget Tax Index. The latter includes the debt that is being acquired by the various levels of government on the grounds that, if the governments' budgets were in fact balanced and no debt were issued, the tax bill would have been higher by the amount of

Table 4.3: The Consumer Tax Index based on 1981 dollars of purchasing power

Year	Real Value of Taxes Paid	Percent Increase in Taxes Paid Over Base Year
1961	$5,300.6	—
1969	$7,851.4	48.1
1972	$9,509.0	79.4
1974	$10,282.2	94.0
1976	$9,505.6	79.3
1978	$11,289.6	113.0
1981	$12,475.0	135.3
1984	$14,005.7	164.2
1986	$11,435.8	115.7
1987	$14,123.7	166.5
1988	$14,651.8	176.4
1989	$14,001.3	164.1
1990	$15,034.2	183.6
1991	$13,457.5	153.9
1992	$13,932.0	162.8

Source: See table 4.1 and Statistics Canada's *Canadian Economic Observer*, 11-210.

the debt issued. The debt issued by such Crown corporations as electric power authorities is not included in this calculation since, in a case of this kind, future electricity rates or other prices—rather than tax rates—will reflect the cost of the debt.

This comparison of the two indices in Table 4.4 and Figure 4.2 shows that if governments were to balance their budgets the tax bill of the average family would be very much higher than it actually is. To the extent that Canadians are made to feel better off by the apparent decline in tax rates, ignoring the accumulating debt acquired by government, they are being subjected to an ongoing fiscal illusion.

Table 4.4: The Consumer Tax Index versus the Balanced Budget Tax Index *(1961=100)*

Year	Consumer Tax Index	Balanced Budget Tax Index
1961	100.0	100.0
1969	186.1	204.3
1972	250.9	281.1
1974	324.1	368.5
1976	357.0	398.4
1978	498.1	581.9
1981	744.8	828.4
1984	1022.6	1368.7
1986	903.9	1135.7
1987	1165.3	1388.5
1988	1257.9	1468.7
1989	1262.2	1463.7
1990	1330.4	1548.9
1991	1342.4	1633.0
1992	1405.2	1641.8

Source: Table 4.5.

Figure 4.2:
The Canadian Consumer Tax Index versus the Balanced Budget Tax Index,
1961-1992

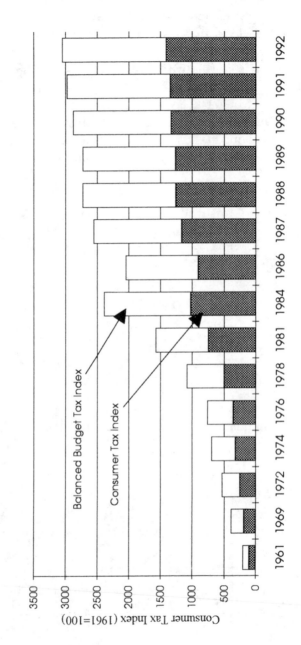

What if we got rid of the debt?

An even more alarming thought experiment is to ask how the average Canadian family's tax index and tax burden would change if all levels of government decided to eliminate their debts by the year 2012— twenty years from now. Assuming a very favourable real income growth rate of 4 percent, population growth of 0.8 percent, and no change in government spending per capita, the average Canadian family's tax bill would rise by $5,450 in the first year to pay off the debt within 20 years. The average family's tax rate would jump from 44 percent in 1992 to 53 percent in 1993 and gradually fall to 28 percent in 2012 as seen in Figure 4.3.

Taxes versus the necessities of life

While the Consumer Tax Index does show the way in which the average family's tax bill has changed over the past 31 years, that information becomes even more significant when it is compared with other major expenditures of the average Canadian family—for shelter, food, and clothing.

Table 4.5 and Figure 4.4 compare the average dollar amount of family cash income, total income before tax, and total taxes paid with family expenditures on other items such as shelter, food, and clothing. It is clear from these figures not only that taxation has become the most significant item that consumers face in their budgets but also that it is growing more rapidly than any other single item. This is made more evident in Table 4.6 and Figure 4.5, which show the various items as indices based on 1961 values. While incomes rose during the period from 1961 to 1992 by 885.5 percent (total income before tax), prices rose 434.6 percent, shelter by 811.3 percent, food expenditures rose 468.8 percent, and clothing 586.4 percent, the tax bill of the average family grew by 1,305.5 percent. The balanced budget tax rate grew even more rapidly, rising by 1,541.8 percent over the same period.

Table 4.7 and Figure 4.6 present the same information expressed as percentages of total income before tax. In this form, the data reveal some interesting comparisons. For example, in 1961 the average family had to use 35.2 percent of its income to provide itself with shelter, food, and

Figure 4.3
Impact of Federal and Provincial Debt Repayment
on the Average Canadian Family
(Tax rate--tax as a percent of cash income)

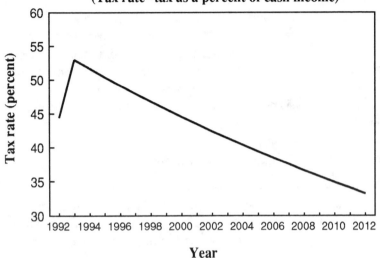

Year

Figure 4.4:
Taxes and Selected Expenditure of the Average
Canadian Family, 1961-1992

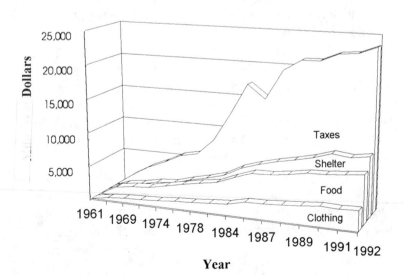

Year

Table 4.5: Income, taxes, and selected expenditures of the average Canadian family (dollars)

Year	Avg. Cash Income	Total Income Before Taxes	Average Taxes Paid		Average Expenditures*		
			Excluding deficit	Including deficit	Shelter	Food	Clothing
1961	$5,000	$7,582	$1,675	$1,675	$977	$1,259	$435
1969	8,000	11,323	3,117	3,422	1,294	1,634	654
1972	10,000	14,154	4,203	4,708	1,778	1,791	739
1974	12,500	17,976	5,429	6,172	1,983	2,320	886
1976	16,500	21,872	5,979	6,673	2,709	2,838	1,119
1978	18,500	27,627	8,343	9,746	3,283	3,319	1,250
1981	26,000	39,236	12,475	13,876	4,009	3,690	1,486
1984	34,216	48,866	17,129	22,926	5,355	4,722	1,659
1986	38,376	55,356	15,141	19,023	6,211	5,626	2,279
1987	41,156	60,599	19,519	23,257	6,840	5,680	2,343
1988	44,192	65,248	21,069	24,600	7,346	6,044	2,501
1989	47,987	67,358	21,142	24,516	7,979	6,498	2,698
1990	50,319	69,788	22,284	25,945	8,785	6,617	2,955
1991	51,092	71,011	22,486	27,352	8,496	6,869	2,859
1992	53,535	74,723	23,537	27,500	8,903	7,161	2,986

Source: Statistics Canada, *Urban Family Expenditure*, 62-549, 62-547, 62-544, 62-537, 62-535, 62-541, 62-525, 62-555, 1990 Family Expenditure Survey; CANTASIM (Fraser Institute Canadian Tax Simulator), July 1992.

*All expenditure items include indirect taxes.

Table 4.6: Indices of income, taxes, and selected expenditures of the average Canadian family *1961=100*

Year	Income		Tax		Consumer Prices	Selected Expenditure*		
	Avg. Cash Income Index	Total Income Before Tax Index	Consumer Tax Index	Consumer Tax Index Incl. Deficits	Avg. CPI	Avg. Shelter Expenditure Index	Avg. Food Expenditure Index	Avg. Clothing Expenditure Index
1961	100.0	100.0	100.0	100.0	100.0	100.0	100.0	100.0
1969	160.0	149.3	186.1	204.3	125.6	132.4	129.8	150.3
1972	200.0	186.7	250.9	281.1	139.9	182.0	142.3	169.9
1974	250.0	237.1	324.1	368.5	167.1	203.0	184.3	203.7
1976	330.0	288.5	357.0	398.4	199.1	277.3	225.4	257.2
1978	370.0	364.4	498.1	581.9	233.9	336.0	263.6	287.4
1981	520.0	517.5	744.8	828.4	316.5	410.3	293.1	341.6
1984	684.3	644.5	1022.6	1368.7	387.0	548.1	375.1	381.4
1986	767.5	730.1	903.9	1135.7	419.0	635.7	446.9	523.9
1987	823.1	799.2	1165.3	1388.5	437.3	700.1	451.2	538.7
1988	883.8	860.6	1257.9	1468.7	455.1	751.9	480.0	574.9
1989	959.7	888.4	1262.2	1463.7	477.8	816.7	516.1	620.2
1990	1006.4	920.4	1330.4	1548.9	469.1	899.2	525.6	679.3
1991	1021.8	936.6	1342.4	1633.0	528.8	869.6	545.6	657.2
1992	1070.7	985.5	1405.2	1641.8	534.6	911.3	568.8	686.4

Percent increase

1961-1992	970.7	885.5	1305.2	1541.8	434.6	811.3	468.8	586.4

Source: Consumer price index data from Statistics Canada, catalogue no. 62-001. The figures in this table are converted to indices by dividing each series in table 4.5 by its value in 1961, and then multiplying that figure by 100.

*All expenditure items include indirect taxes.

Figure 4.5

How the Consumer Tax Index (CTI) has Increased Relative to Other Selected Indices, 1961-1992

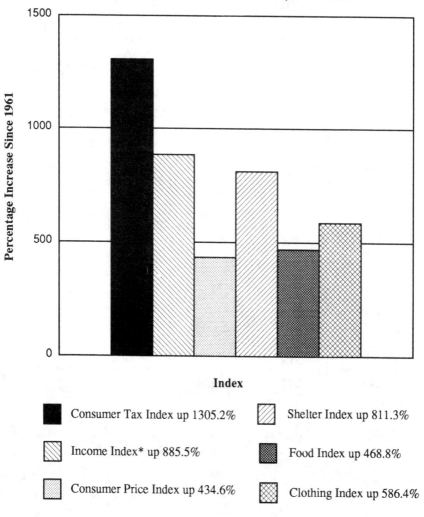

Consumer Tax Index up 1305.2%

Shelter Index up 811.3%

Income Index* up 885.5%

Food Index up 468.8%

Consumer Price Index up 434.6%

Clothing Index up 586.4%

* Total Income Before Tax Index

Source: Table 4.6.

Table 4.7: Taxes and selected expenditures of the average Canadian family expressed as a percentage of total income before tax

Year	Taxes	Selected Expenditure*		
		Shelter	Food	Clothing
1961	22.1%	12.9%	16.6%	5.7%
1969	27.5	11.4	14.4	5.8
1972	29.7	12.6	12.7	5.2
1974	30.2	11.0	12.9	4.9
1976	27.3	12.4	13.0	5.1
1978	30.2	11.9	12.0	4.5
1981	31.8	10.2	9.4	3.8
1984	35.1	11.0	9.7	3.4
1986	27.4	11.2	10.2	4.1
1987	32.2	11.3	9.4	3.9
1988	32.3	11.3	9.3	3.8
1989	31.4	11.8	9.6	4.0
1990	31.9	12.6	9.5	4.2
1991	31.7	12.0	9.7	4.0
1992	31.5	11.9	9.6	4.0

Source: Table 4.5.

*All selected expenditure items include indirect taxes.

clothing. In the same year, 22.1 percent of the family's income went to government in the form of taxes.

By 1974 the situation had been reversed, and 30.2 percent of income went to satisfy the taxman, while only 29 percent was required to provide the family with shelter, food and clothing.

Figure 4.6
Taxes and Selected Expenditures of the Average Canadian Family Expressed as a Percentage of Total Income Before Tax

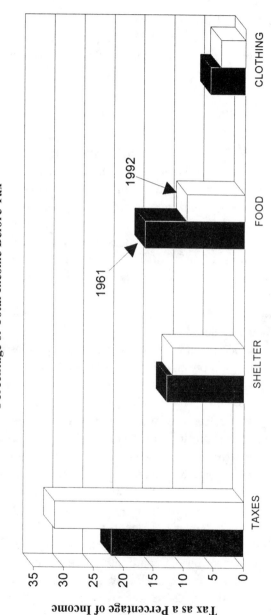

By 1992 the situation had worsened significantly. Whereas the proportion of income consumed by taxes continued to increase, the fraction of income spent on necessities (shelter, food, and clothing) dropped dramatically. The average family spent 25.5 percent of its income on the necessities of life while 31.5 percent of their income went to the taxman.

The average burden of tax versus the average family's tax burden

This chapter has dealt exclusively with the tax position of the "average" family. To some extent the conclusions of such an analysis can be misleading, because of the exclusive focus on the average family. In the next chapter this weakness is corrected by discussing the tax position of "un-average" Canadians. Similarly, it is possible to mistake the average family's burden for another measure which is sometimes used, that of the average tax burden of all Canadian families. Before leaving discussion of the average family's tax burden, therefore, it is important to establish and understand the differences between these two measures.

In this chapter, the tax burden of the average family has been calculated by selecting an average-income family and calculating that family's theoretical tax burden from the tax tables. In this regard it is interesting to note that the average family in 1992 has an income of $53,535 and that the family pays $9,106 in income tax or 38.7 percent of its total tax bill. The remaining $14,431 or 61.3 percent is made up of other taxes such as sales and property taxes. Another way of calculating an average tax burden would be to add up all the taxes in the economy and simply divide that total tax figure by total incomes in the economy. This would produce an average tax rate for all Canadian families. Such a calculation is displayed in Table 4.8 along with the average family's tax rate. This table also shows what the tax rates would have been if the deficits incurred by governments were included.

It is quite clear from the table that the average family's tax rate is below that faced by all Canadians in the economy as a whole. Moreover, as the analysis in the next chapter shows, the tax rate faced by the average family is considerably lower than the tax rates faced by families whose incomes are above average. Similarly, much of the total tax bill is collected from families whose incomes are above the average.

It is this "progressivity" of the tax structure which produces the difference between the two average tax calculations—the more progressive the tax system the greater the difference. Progressivity is the subject of discussion in the next chapter.

Table 4.8: Average tax rates for all Canadian families versus tax rates of the average Canadian family (percent)

Year	Average Canadian Family's Tax Rate		Average Tax Rate For All Canadian Families	
	Excluding Deficit	Including Deficit	Excluding Deficit	Including Deficit
1961	22.1	22.1	25.2	25.2
1969	27.5	30.2	31.1	34.3
1972	29.7	33.3	31.6	35.3
1974	30.2	34.3	33.3	37.8
1976	27.3	30.5	31.8	35.9
1978	30.2	35.3	31.0	35.0
1981	31.8	35.4	32.9	35.7
1984	35.1	46.9	30.9	41.3
1986	27.4	34.4	31.0	38.9
1987	32.2	38.4	31.9	38.0
1988	32.3	37.7	31.7	37.0
1989	31.4	36.4	31.8	36.8
1990	31.9	37.2	32.6	38.0
1991	31.7	38.5	31.9	34.7
1992	31.5	36.8	31.9	37.3

Source: Fraser Institute Canadian Tax Simulator (CANTSIM).

Chapter 5

The Relative Burden
of Tax

IN CHAPTER 4 WE INVESTIGATED the tax burden of the average Canadian family and how that burden has changed through time. While that view of the tax system has some inherent interest, it represents a very particular aspect of a much larger picture. The purpose of this chapter is to analyze this larger picture—to examine all income groups and how their relative income and tax positions have changed between 1961 and 1992.

The distribution of income

In order to analyze the relative income and tax positions of Canadians, we have divided all Canadian families into three income groups. The lowest group consists of the bottom three income deciles. The middle group consists of the next four deciles, and the upper group of the top three deciles. An income decile is what one gets when arranging families according to total income before tax from lowest to highest and then selecting the first 10 percent (lowest incomes), the second 10 percent, and so on. The resulting grouping of families is presented in Table 5.1 and illustrated in Figure 5.1.

Table 5.1: Decile distribution of income (income before tax) (percent)

Year	Income groups		
	Lower 3 deciles	Middle 4 deciles	Upper 3 deciles
1961	10.80	35.60	53.60
1972	9.00	33.10	57.90
1976	8.80	31.70	59.50
1981	9.70	34.50	55.80
1984	9.52	33.64	56.84
1987	9.63	33.82	56.65
1992	9.22	33.20	57.58

Source: Fraser Institute Canadian Tax Simulator (CANTASIM).

Figure 5.1
Percent of Total Income Before Taxes earned by Lower, Middle, and Upper Income Groups, 1961-1992

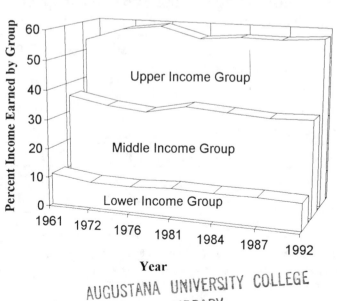

The table reveals that the relative shares of the different income groups have been remarkably constant over the period since 1961. In evaluating this result, the reader should bear in mind that the data have a variety of aspects that make them susceptible to misinterpretation. First of all, the data fail to make any allowance for the age of the individuals. This is an important fact, since age is a principal determinant of income. Young people first entering the labour market typically earn wages or salaries considerably below the average and considerably below what will be their own life time average. Similarly, elderly people who have passed the age of retirement are typically in a phase of their lives when their incomes are considerably below their lifetime average and when they are spending the savings and pensions of their working lifetime.

For example, Table 5.2 displays the "life-cycle average expected wage" for a Canadian male in 1989. Two sources of data on the earnings profile are available—information from taxation statistics and Statistics Canada's income surveys. While the two sources yield different estimates, they both show the expected age-related movement in wages relative to the average.

Table 5.2: Income in age groups as a percentage of average for all groups, Canadian males, 1989

Age	Taxation Statistics Data	Statistics Canada Income Survey Data	Average Profile
Under 25	0.445	0.622	0.533
25-34	0.925	1.017	0.971
35-44	1.229	1.338	1.283
45-54	1.348	1.456	1.402
55-64	1.216	0.045	0.630
65 & over	0.883	0.825	0.854

Source: Statistics Canada, *Income Distribution by Size in Canada, 1989*, catalogue no. 13-207; *Taxation Statistics*, 1991 edition, "Analysing Returns for the 1989 Taxation Year and Miscellaneous Statistics," summary table 4.

Failure to account for the age of income earners can lead to a considerably distorted impression of how income distribution is changing—particularly if there are dramatic changes in the age structure of the population as there have been in Canada. In future years, as the number of people in or near retirement grows, it can be expected that the distribution of income will be affected. More of the population will be elderly and more of the population will have lower incomes as a result. Evidently, this will not mean that the population is, in any sense, worse off.

A second important warning for those who would draw from these data conclusions about the "equity" of the income distribution is that they ignore income-in-kind that people receive from government. Housing, medical care, education, and other services which are received as direct benefits from government, rather than in the form of cash payments, are not reflected in the income distribution table. And the public provision of these services potentially represents one of the most significant redistributive aspects of Canadian society.

For these reasons it would be inappropriate to infer from the data in Table 5.1 that there had been no change in the effective distribution of income since 1961. The data in their present form are incapable of providing meaningful answers to that question. What the data do provide is a yardstick against which to measure the distribution of taxes. They will allow us to infer whether, for example, groups of people with low incomes bear a disproportionate share of the tax burden. They will provide an indication of the progressivity or regressivity of the Canadian tax burden. In order to arrive at these results, it is necessary to combine income results with those on tax distribution which are the subject of the next section.

Tax distribution and tax rates

Our measurements of the distribution of the tax burden provide some interesting and, indeed, puzzling results for the tax distribution. Whereas up until the mid '70s there had been a more or less steady increase in the tax burden borne by the upper third of income groups (that is to say, the top three income deciles), during the interval 1976 to 1981, the share of the top group fell markedly. As can be seen from Table 5.3 and Figure 5.2, during 1976 the top three income deciles accounted for fully 66.5 percent of the total tax payments. By 1981 this had fallen to 61.3 percent of the total, a decrease of 5.2 percentage points. The decline in the tax burden borne by the top three income deciles was matched by a corresponding increase in the tax burden faced by the

Table 5.3: Decile distribution of taxes (percent)

Year	Lower 3 deciles	Middle 4 deciles	Upper 3 deciles
1961	8.5	30.6	60.9
1972	6.0	30.0	64.0
1976	6.2	27.3	66.5
1981	6.2	32.5	61.3
1984	5.5	32.9	61.6
1987	5.5	32.3	62.2
1992	5.8	31.4	62.8

Source: Fraser Institute Canadian Tax Simulator (CANTASIM).

Figure 5.2
Percent of Total Taxes Paid by Income Group, 1961-1992

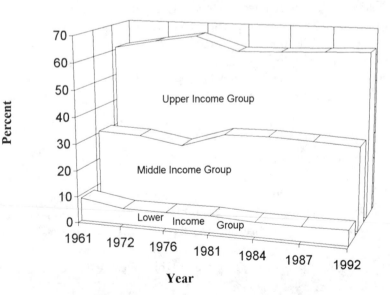

middle income deciles. For example, the fourth to seventh income deciles which had borne 27.3 percent of the total tax burden in 1976, by 1981 were bearing 32.5 percent—an increase of 5.2 percentage points. Since 1981 there has been a slight decrease in the tax borne by the lower two income groups and a rise by the upper income group.

As Table 5.4 shows, there had been a very modest shift in the incidence of the personal income tax system away from the lower income deciles and toward the upper income deciles. The top three income groups accounted for 68.7 percent of total income tax payments in 1981 up from 67.8 percent in 1976. By 1992, the top three income groups accounted for only 65.7 percent of total income tax payments.

Table 5.4: Decile distribution of personal income tax (percent)

Year	Lower 3 deciles	Middle 4 deciles	Upper 3 deciles
1976	2.7	29.5	67.8
1981	1.9	29.4	68.7
1984	2.5	30.9	66.6
1987	2.6	28.8	68.6
1992	4.2	30.1	65.7

Source: Fraser Institute Canadian Tax Simulator (CANTASIM).

A major factor explaining variations in the share of taxes paid by the top three deciles has been the change in the incidence of the capital-related taxes. These are chiefly property taxes and corporate profit taxes. As Table 5.5 shows, the change in the pattern of these capital-related taxes has been truly astounding. Between 1976 and 1981 the burden of property taxes for the top three deciles dropped from 71.9 to 54.0 percent. The burden crept up to 53.7 percent in 1984 and rose dramatically after 1987.

Analysis of the underlying factors reveals that part of the reason for the dramatic shift in the incidence of the capital taxes has been the change in the distribution of capital income amongst Canadians which

Table 5.5: Decile distribution of profit taxes and property taxes (percent)

Year	Decile distribution of profit taxes		
	Lower Income Group	Middle Income Group	Upper Income Group
1976	10.30	17.80	71.90
1981	12.20	31.80	56.00
1984	10.99	35.33	53.68
1987	11.63	36.82	51.55
1992	5.52	27.48	67.00
	Decile distribution of property taxes		
	Lower Income Group	Middle Income Group	Upper Income Group
1976	10.30	17.80	71.90
1981	13.00	33.00	54.00
1984	10.99	35.33	53.68
1987	11.64	36.81	51.55
1992	5.47	27.22	67.31

Source: Fraser Institute Canadian Tax Simulator (CANTASIM).

is described in table 5.6. But another reason why capital taxes fell for the upper income deciles in the late '70s and early '80s, and then rose in the late '80s and early '90s, is probably due to changes in exemptions. For example, in the early 1980s Canadians took advantage of the tax preferences which the government inserted in the tax system to encourage the development of various sectors of the economy such as oil exploration, rental housing, and Canadian films. The tax reform of 1987 effectively put an end to much of the tax preference game.

Table 5.6: Decile distribution of capital income (percent)

Year	Lower 3 deciles	Middle 4 deciles	Upper 3 deciles
1976	10.3	17.8	71.9
1981	13.0	33.0	54.0
1984	10.7	34.3	55.0
1987	11.5	35.6	52.9
1992	5.5	26.80	67.6

Source: Fraser Institute Canadian Tax Simulator (CANTASIM).

One factor which underlies all of the distribution series is the massive surge in the number of individuals in the upper income classes. In 1978, for example, only 10.0 percent of the population had an income of $35,000 or more. By 1988, 45.8 percent of the population enjoyed an income at least as large as that. While of course inflation has played a role in this development, some of this increase is the result of an increasing number of families containing two income earners whose joint income pushes the family into the higher bracket. The implication of this for the distribution of taxation among families is that families in the upper income deciles seem to be paying less and less tax because they are composed increasingly of individuals with lower incomes.

As noted in Chapter 2, two incomes totalling, say, $30,000 are taxed less in total (by the income tax structure) than one income of $30,000. Since upper income families are increasingly composed of two income earners, this has put downward pressure on the average tax rate in this income range. And, during the 1974-1992 period, the number of two income earner families included in the top income brackets has increased.

One feature of the developments has been the reversal of trends established in 1976. From then until 1984 the percentage of total income earned by the upper income groups had been steadily decreasing with the middle income groups gaining ground. This is quite clearly reflected in Table 5.1 which shows the distribution of income by population decile. Whereas in 1976 nearly 60 percent of all income was earned by the top three deciles, this had dropped to 55.8 percent by 1981. However, by 1992 the upper three deciles had rebounded to claim 57.58 percent of income. Whether or not this is the start of a new trend is too early to tell. One further implication of the distribution of total taxes (as opposed to the distribution of income taxes) is interesting to note. The flatness in the tax distribution which began to emerge in the late 1970s was reversed in 1984 as a sharper progressivity developed.

Who pays the tax bill?

As can be seen from Table 5.3, the largest portion of the tax burden ultimately settles on the higher income groups. In 1992, the top 30 percent of families paid nearly 63 percent of all taxes. Of course, while the tax burden fell disproportionately on the top 30 percent of families, that group also received a substantial fraction of the income. In 1992, the top 30 percent earned 57.6 percent. While this was down from the 59.5 percent of the total earned in 1976, it is larger than the 53.6 percent share this group received in 1961.

In 1992 the top 30 percent of income earners had an average cash income of $100,885 and included all families whose incomes were above $63,853. (This compares to an average income of $32,615 in 1976 and an entry income of $21,494 in that year.)

The rags-to-riches tax burden

The notion that a tax system may discourage people from improving their income situation suggests the value of calculating the extent to which Canadians' individual tax situations would have changed during the 1961 to 1992 period if their relative incomes had increased. Table 5.7 presents the results of a tax analysis for a hypothetical Canadian individual whose cash income grew at a constant rate from half the average in 1961 to twice the average in 1992. This "Horatio Alger's" income grew from $2,750 in 1961 to $107,070 in 1992.

In 1961, a total income of $4,776 attracted a tax bill of $960, or an average tax rate of total income of 20.1 percent. By 1972, the hypothetical income earner had a total income of $10,084 and paid taxes of $3,821, or a tax rate of 23.6 percent. Finally, in 1992, when cash income was $107,070, total income was $149,446, and taxes paid amounted to

$47,074. Thus, the average tax rate on total income had risen to 31.5 percent. In each case the tax calculation does not include the amount of debt accumulated by government on behalf of the taxpayer. Including debt, the increase in tax burden is even more dramatic, as can be seen in Table 5.7.

Over the thirty-one year period 1961-1992, the hypothetical Horatio experienced a 3,029.8 percent increase in total income. Over the same period, taxes paid increased by 4,803.5 percent excluding debt. Including debt they increased 5,629.2 percent.

Table 5.7: The rags-to-riches tax burden

1961	1969	1972	1976	1980	1986	1992	% Increase 1961-1992
Cash Income ($)							
2,750	7,075	10,084	16,175	25,945	52,706	107,070	3793.5
Total Income Before Tax ($)							
4,775	11,612	16,205	25,270	39,407	76,742	149,446	3029.8
Tax Excluding Deficit ($)							
960	2,621	3,821	6,313	10,433	22,161	47,074	4803.5
Tax Including Deficit ($)							
960	2,878	4,280	7,046	11,604	27,843	55,000	5629.2
Tax Rate on Total Income Excluding Deficit (%)							
20.1	22.6	23.6	25.0	26.5	28.9	31.5	56.7
Tax Rate on Total Income Including Deficit (%)							
20.1	24.8	26.4	27.9	29.4	36.3	36.8	83.1

Source: Fraser Institute Canadian Tax Simulator (CANTASIM).

N.b.: Assumed income was arrived at by assuming income increased smoothly in equal percentage increases from the poverty level in 1961 to high income in 1992.

Meanwhile, the tax rate faced by the individual increased 56.7 percent. In improving their circumstances, Canadian Horatio Algers would have earned a total income over the period of $939,067 and paid total taxes of $391,749.

Marginal versus average tax rates

Tax rates discourage effort at every point in the income scale. Perversely, this effect is most pronounced for the poor! The reason for this bizarre result is that many social assistance payments stop abruptly once the recipient starts earning income. In effect, the tax rate on the first few dollars of earned income can be large. This tax rate is referred to by economists as the "marginal tax rate" meaning the rate one experiences as one moves up in income. It can differ dramatically from the average tax rate, which is the one we are most accustomed to thinking about. Table 5.8 shows both marginal and average rates for different income levels for Canada and Figure 5.3 illustrates these.

It is this marginal rate which enters into people's calculations. When people decides whether or not to work an extra hour, they asks themselves how much extra they will earn, and how much extra tax they will pay. They do not consider how much tax on average they are paying because this does not reflect the true return to any extra effort they may wish to provide. As the table shows, these rates jump as one moves from the second to the third income decile, reflecting that initially it is very costly to work, because one rapidly loses social assistance. This effect fades in the middle income brackets but rises again at higher levels of income as the effect of rapidly increasing progressivity starts to be felt. Surprisingly, marginal rates flatten out at the upper end of the income scale. This probably is due to the tax reforms of the late 1980s which eliminated sharply progressive tax brackets as well as the many exemptions available to the upper end of the income scale.

Table 5.8: Average and marginal tax rates, Canada, 1992

Average Tax Rates (percent)

	Lower Income Groups				Middle Income Groups				Upper Income Groups	
1	2	3	4	5	6	7	8	9	10
(Income Measure=Cash Income)									
18.83	20.10	32.36	34.10	40.48	43.84	45.51	47.06	48.50	51.24
(Income Measure=Total Income Before Tax)									
14.98	16.31	24.17	25.46	29.28	31.29	32.45	33.38	34.29	35.70

Marginal Tax Rates (percent)

1-2*	2-3	3-4	4-5	5-6	6-7	7-8	8-9	9-10
(Income Measure=Cash Income)								
21.27	66.41	39.97	69.30	60.60	54.17	54.81	54.34	55.53
(Income Measure=Total Income Before Tax)								
17.58	40.61	29.80	43.92	40.56	38.46	37.86	37.98	37.83

*Marginal tax rate faced when you move from the first to the second decile.

Source: Fraser Institute Canadian Tax Simulator (CANTASIM).

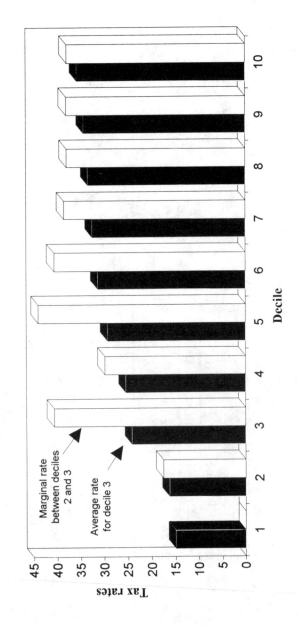

Figure 5.3
Average and Marginal Tax Rates by Income Decile, 1992

Chapter 6

Taxes Across Canada

IN THIS CHAPTER, WE EXTEND the analysis of the preceding sections to focus on particular provinces.

Table 6.1 presents the tax situation for the average family by province of residence. Average family in this context is taken to mean a family unit which has an average income for the province of residence. Thus, for example, the average family in Newfoundland has an income of $47,900 in 1992, whereas the average family in Ontario has an income of $62,121, and so on. It is very interesting to survey the results for each of these families and to see just how the tax bill varies from province to province, and from category to category. It is particularly interesting to see which provinces have the highest propensity to tax in each of the tax categories. Income tax comprises between 33.9 percent and 42.3 percent of the family's tax bill. The highest rate is in Alberta, where the average family faces a 17 percent income tax rate on cash income, and the lowest in Manitoba at 14.7 percent. The sales tax is more heavily relied upon in the Maritimes than in the rest of Canada. 24.3 cents out of each tax dollar paid in taxes by the average Newfoundland family are collected in sales tax. By comparison 14.9 cents out of each tax dollar are collected in sales tax from the average Ontario family and 8.9 cents

Table 6.1: Taxes of the average family by province, 1992 (dollars)*

Province	Avg. Cash Income	Total Income Before Tax	Profits Tax	Income Tax	Sales Tax	Liquor, Tobacco, Amusement & Other Excise Taxes	Auto, Fuel, & Motor Vehicle Licence Taxes	Social Security, Pension, Medical & Hospital Taxes	Property Tax	Natural Resources Taxes	Import Duties	Other Taxes	Total Taxes
NFLD	$47,900	$64,992	$726	$6,308	$4,349	$1,200	$731	$2,626	$540	$136	$389	$865	$17,870
PEI	40,488	54,643	809	5,140	3,175	1,149	623	2,100	860	17	355	151	14,380
NS	43,019	59,247	788	7,379	3,415	1,119	699	2,727	936	26	443	411	17,944
NB	45,650	6,1617	573	6,749	3,820	1,074	785	2,786	841	18	410	238	17,294
QUE	47,761	67,736	996	8,129	4,038	1,006	694	4,620	1,228	22	490	584	21,808
ONT	62,121	86,679	1,643	10,846	4,128	1,167	784	4,786	2,440	56	600	1,334	27,784
MAN	49,550	70,806	1,964	7,265	3,067	1,236	621	2,675	3,461	293	475	392	21,450
SASK	48,470	68,275	1,563	7,148	3,260	1,277	1,104	2,396	2,022	860	459	454	20,542
ALTA	53,927	73,851	988	9,153	1,925	1,466	708	3,767	1,443	1330	562	322	21,664
BC	53,706	73,786	1,261	9,953	3,674	1,487	663	3,821	1,466	645	578	584	24,133
CDA	53,535	74,723	1,267	9,106	3,748	1,180	738	4,171	1,748	259	533	787	23,537

Source: Statistics Canada data on taxes and income; provincial and federal government budgets and public accounts; Fraser Institute Canadian Tax Simulator (CANTASIM).
*Preliminary estimates (June, 1992).

from the average Albertan family which has no provincial sales tax. Manitoba charges more than other provinces do for property tax, collecting 16.1 percent of taxes in this form, whereas Newfoundland only collects 3.0 percent of its taxes as property tax. Saskatchewan, Alberta and British Columbia reap more from natural resource revenues than do other provinces. In Alberta, for example, petroleum-related taxes are not collected directly from the tax paying public; rather, they are collected indirectly from the corporations that recover oil and gas from the ground. It is nevertheless the case that the oil and gas in the ground in Alberta belongs to the people of Alberta. It is appropriate, therefore, to regard the taxes which are paid as a result of exploitation of these petroleum resources as the income of Albertans, and hence a tax on Albertans.

While this is the appropriate technical treatment of petroleum resource taxes it does confuse somewhat the inter-provincial comparison of tax burdens. If we subtracted from the $21,664 total tax bill the average Albertan family faces, the $1,330 which are collected on their behalf from the petroleum industry, we find that the total tax bill is reduced to $20,334 for the average family. A similar adjustment for natural resource revenues has been made for both Saskatchewan and British Columbia. The bracketed figures in table 6.2 represent the tax rate calculated on a basis which excludes the natural resource taxes.

In comparing these tax results for the various provinces, it is important to remember that the standard of comparison is the average family. That is to say, the family in each province whose income is average. It is, therefore, the case that the individuals in different provinces will have different incomes since the average income in each province varies considerably. And, some of the differences in tax burden between the provinces is due to nothing more than the differences in income.

Table 6.3 provides a distribution of taxes by province according to population decile. The great benefit of this table is that it is independent of the incomes within each province, and makes possible a comparison of the provinces according to how the tax burden is spread within each among the various income groups. The outcome of this analysis is noteworthy; there seems to be very little variation between the provinces in the extent of the progressivity or regressivity of their tax

Table 6.2: Provincial tax rates* as a percentage of cash income and total income before tax, 1992 (percent)

Province	Cash Income		Total Income Before Tax	
	Excluding Deficit	Including Deficit	Excluding Deficit	Including Deficit
NFLD	37.31	43.09	27.50	31.76
PEI	35.52	39.57	26.32	29.32
NS	41.71	49.56	30.29	35.99
NB	37.88	44.70	28.07	33.12
QUE	45.66	52.99	32.20	37.37
ONT	44.73	52.62	32.05	37.71
MAN	43.29	48.70	30.29	34.08
SASK	42.38	49.05	30.09	34.82
SASK**	40.61	47.00	28.83	33.37
ALTA	40.17	47.16	29.34	34.44
ALTA**	37.71	44.27	27.53	32.32
BC	44.94	51.24	32.71	37.29
BC**	43.74	49.87	31.83	36.30
CDA	43.97	51.37	31.50	36.80

* For the family with average income in 1992 in each of the provinces.

** These the tax rates resulting when natural resource taxes are removed from the average family's tax bill.

Source: Fraser Institute Canadian Tax Simulator (CANTASIM).

systems. That is to say, the upper income groups tend to absorb a little over 60 percent of the total tax bill, with some minor variations.

The stability of the distribution series in each of the provinces is especially remarkable considering that each province relies so differently on the various forms of taxation. This fact, which was pointed out above in the discussion of Table 6.1, ought to provide some variation in the tax rates unless, of course, the differences in the progressivity and regressivity of the various tax rates offset each other. From Table 6.3 it appears that the various tax measures offset the rate of progressivity of the provincial tax systems.

Table 6.3: Decile distribution of taxes by province, 1992 (percent)

Province	Lower 3 deciles	Middle 4 deciles	Upper 3 deciles
NFLD	8.05	32.21	59.74
PEI	6.07	28.05	65.89
NS	4.75	30.61	64.64
NB	5.54	31.38	63.08
QUE	5.19	31.64	63.17
ONT	6.31	33.33	60.36
MAN	5.82	31.51	62.67
SASK	5.30	29.76	64.94
ALTA	5.60	30.16	64.24
BC	6.32	32.52	61.16
CDA	5.79	31.43	62.78

Source: Fraser Institute Canadian Tax Simulator (CANTASIM).

However, as Table 6.4 shows, there are some important differences between the tax systems in the various provinces. Table 6.4 highlights these differences in the form of the average tax rates which are payable by the various income deciles in the different provinces. Thus, for example, in Newfoundland the lowest income decile paid a tax rate of

Table 6.4: Average tax rates by decile by province, 1992
(Income measure = total income before tax) (percent)

Province	Lower Income Groups (Deciles)				Middle Income Groups (Deciles)				Upper Income Groups (Deciles)		
	1	2	3	4	5	6	7	8	9	10
NFLD	15.22	15.76	21.68	22.57	21.10	26.22	30.50	31.00	30.95	33.34
PEI	12.23	17.61	18.35	25.51	17.63	24.46	27.40	30.10	31.95	33.68
NS	13.34	13.67	18.34	20.99	25.25	29.88	31.03	32.01	33.94	34.28
NB	10.72	13.90	20.69	21.51	25.54	27.91	29.65	32.03	32.17	33.57
QUE	11.97	15.65	22.18	25.46	27.91	31.51	33.51	34.66	35.45	36.84
ONT	17.51	18.26	25.73	29.37	30.94	31.88	32.90	33.84	33.98	36.05
MAN	12.88	16.08	21.44	23.09	25.96	28.49	30.58	30.94	31.59	34.26
SASK	16.11	18.81	18.14	25.12	24.31	29.43	30.85	33.18	35.22	35.82
ALTA	14.73	18.38	20.63	24.84	25.92	28.51	30.52	31.21	33.05	35.70
BC	15.67	18.58	25.35	25.55	29.71	32.19	32.44	32.88	34.34	35.42
CDA	14.98	16.31	24.17	25.46	29.28	31.29	32.45	33.38	34.29	35.70

Source: Fraser Institute Canadian Tax Simulator (CANTASIM).

15.22 percent on average, whereas the top decile paid a tax rate of 33.34 percent. In Quebec, on the other hand, the top decile paid 36.84 percent, whereas the bottom decile paid 11.97 percent.

Accounting for the future tax burden

During the last year, it has become increasingly obvious that the tax comparison between provinces has a major defect. Namely, those provinces which relied less on taxes and more on borrowing to finance their expenditures would appear to have a less intrusive taxation system. The reason, as we have discussed in previous chapters, is because deficits force the burden of the taxes needed to finance current expenditures onto future generations of taxpayers. A measure of taxation which ignores this shifting of the tax burden cannot provide an accurate picture of the true fiscal stance of a government. Therefore, we have created a provincial distribution of tax burdens based on the total tax consequences of the current expenditures of government—that is, including the deficits which governments incur. The data are presented in Table 6.5.

It is clear from these data, and the compilations included in Table 6.2 and Figure 6.1, which show tax rates by province including the deficit levels, that there is significant reliance on taxing future generations by all jurisdictions.

Underlying this pattern of taxation is a pattern of expenditures. That is, the reason for raising revenues is to pay for government spending. Accordingly an alternative, and perhaps more direct measure of the level of government activity, is the level of government spending. Table 6.6 presents provincial government spending levels in each of the provinces both in total dollar terms and per capita terms adjusted for the amount of that spending which is financed by federal equalization payments. These figures do not include other types of federal government spending by province and the impression given by the figures may be misleading to the extent that there is a differential in the level of spending activity by the federal government in the various provinces.

Even though there may be some difficulties with the calculations, they reveal a very interesting pattern of spending and suggest interesting comparisons with the taxation data. Quebec, Ontario, Alberta and British Columbia are among the highest spending and highest taxing

Table 6.5: Taxes of the average family including deficits* by province, 1992 (dollars)

Province	Avg. Cash Income	Total Income Before Tax	Profits Tax	Income Tax	Sales Tax	Liquor, Tobacco, Amusement & Other Excise Taxes	Auto, Fuel, & Motor Vehicle Licence Taxes	Social Security, Pension, Medical & Hospital Taxes	Property Tax	Natural Resources Taxes	Import Duties	Other Taxes	Total Taxes
NFLD	$47,900	$64,992	$838	$7,285	$5,023	$1,386	$845	$3,033	$623	$157	$449	$999	$20,639
PEI	40,488	54,643	902	5,728	3,538	1,280	694	2,341	958	19	396	168	16,023
NS	43,019	59,247	937	8,768	4,058	1,330	831	3,240	1,113	31	526	489	21,322
NB	45,650	6,1617	676	7,963	4,507	1,267	926	3,287	993	21	484	281	20,405
QUE	47,761	67,736	1,156	9,435	4,687	1,167	805	5,362	1,426	26	569	678	25,310
ONT	62,121	86,679	1,933	12,761	4,857	1,373	923	5,631	2,871	66	706	1,569	32,690
MAN	49,550	70,806	2,209	8,173	3,451	1,391	699	3,009	3,894	330	534	441	24,131
SASK	48,470	68,275	1,809	8,273	3,773	1,478	1,277	2,773	2,340	995	531	525	23,776
ALTA	53,927	73,851	1,160	10,745	2,260	1,721	832	4,422	1,694	1,561	660	378	25,433
BC	53,706	73,786	1,438	11,349	4,189	1,696	756	4,357	1,672	735	659	666	27,517
CDA	53,535	74,723	1,480	10,639	4,379	1,379	862	4,874	2,042	302	623	920	27,500

*Federal and provincial government deficits.

Source: Statistics Canada data on taxes and income; provincial and federal government budgets and public accounts; Fraser Institute Canadian Tax Simulator (CANTASIM).

Table 6.6: Total spending and spending per capita by province, 1992

Province	Total Spending (Millions $)	Spending per Capita ($)	Equalization Payments per Capita ($)	Adjusted per Capita Spending ($)	Rank by Spending	Rank by Taxation
NFLD	$3,536.9	$6,159.7	$1,645.8	$4,514.0	5	9
PEI	749.8	5,776.9	1,579.4	4,197.5	8	10
NS	4,784.4	5,280.3	1,104.5	4,175.7	9	6
NB	4,095.6	5,636.0	1,286.6	4,349.3	7	8
QUE	40,703.0	5,902.9	620.6	5,282.4	2	1
ONT	50,947.0	5,085.1	0.0	5,085.1	4	3
MAN	5,450.0	4,980.8	991.6	3,989.2	10	4
SASK	5,008.8	5,047.7	604.7	4,443.0	6	5
ALTA	13,273.3	5,206.2	0.0	5,206.2	3	7
BC	17,980.0	5,493.4	0.0	5,493.4	1	2

Source: Fraser Institute Canadian Tax Simulator (CANTASIM).

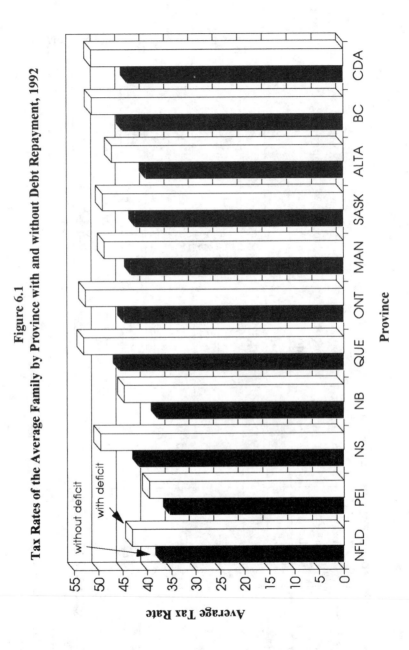

Figure 6.1

Tax Rates of the Average Family by Province with and without Debt Repayment, 1992

provinces, while the Maritimes are among the lowest taxing and lowest spending jurisdictions.

Marginal tax rates and the persistence of poverty

In the previous chapter we mentioned that it is marginal tax rates which discourage productive efforts. Table 6.7 ranks the provinces on their marginal tax rates in the first three income deciles and compares their poverty rates based on Statistics Canada's Low Income Cut-offs (1986 base). There appears to be a strong link. While such broad aggregates cannot prove that high tax rates are a cause of poverty, they point to an area that needs further study and may be one piece in the puzzle of why many are "trapped" in low incomes.

Table 6.7: Marginal tax rates, poverty rates, and low income groups, 1992

Percentage of families below LICO in the first 3 deciles

Province	Decile		
	1	2	3
NFLD	50.92%	29.52%	11.03%
PEI	55.13	26.47	14.01
NS	48.30	30.46	16.16
NB	50.92	30.47	14.03
QUE	43.32	28.83	17.92
ONT	59.92	31.20	6.47
MAN	46.59	27.62	15.06
SASK	51.11	24.46	18.37
ALTA	48.70	26.98	17.55
BC	52.92	27.38	12.21
CDA	50.72	29.02	13.54

Table 6.7: (continued)

Province	Marginal Tax Rates (percent)		
	Deciles 1-2*	Deciles 2-3	Deciles 3-4
NFLD	19.71%	61.56%	34.20%
PEI	27.88	25.81	78.10
NS	16.61	43.85	39.21
NB	20.39	55.05	31.29
QUE	23.40	59.91	52.23
ONT	23.45	63.25	61.72
MAN	23.91	55.48	39.62
SASK	26.54	19.35	71.66
ALTA	27.05	35.75	53.77
BC	26.52	65.73	33.08
CDA	21.27	66.41	39.97

Source: Fraser Institute Canadian Tax Simulator (CANTASIM).
*Marginal tax rate faced when move from the first to the second decile.

Chapter 7

Who Pays the Corporate Tax?

Introduction

CORPORATIONS ARE A MAJOR SOURCE of revenue for federal and provincial governments. In 1991 they paid $15.0 billion in taxes, 6.2 percent of all government takings. These statements are factually correct, but misleading. "Corporations" do not really bear these taxes, people do. The purpose of this chapter is to ask "which people?" Even though we are well furnished with data on how much corporations pay and who owns them, answering who pays the corporate tax is not a straightforward exercise. A tax on corporations is a tax on capital. When the tax rises, capital will flee and this will affect what capital and labour earn and what consumers pay. Who truly ends up bearing the tax depends on these aftershocks. Our calculations suggest that the elderly bear the brunt.

Background

A corporation is a group of people bound by contract to work together and to share the spoils of that work. In its simplest terms it is a joint venture between capitalists and workers. This view is too coarse to be of much help in explaining why corporations exist and the many subtle incentives they respond to, but it is all we need for the present discussion. The corporate tax falls directly on profits. Profits are what is left over after labour and interest on capital as well as materials costs have been paid, and this residual can be thought of as going to capitalists. This is why the corporate tax is a tax on capital. There is often confusion over what the corporate tax rate is because as well as having their profits taxed, corporations may receive special tax breaks which allow them to write off more than their true capital expenses. This means a corporation may pay a high statutory rate on its profits but at a much lower actual rate because of its deductions.

Statutory rates on capital had risen in the 1970s and '80s but revenue from the corporate tax was unsteady because profits varied, and deductions had increased, thereby "eroding the tax base." It is a general principle of taxation that if you want to raise a certain amount of revenue you distort people's choices less by imposing a low tax on a broad base than a high tax on a narrow base. By the mid 1980s the base had become too narrow and this prompted the first stage of corporate tax reform. In the 1986 budget the federal government started phasing out deductions such as the inventory allowance and the investment tax credit, and announced a leisurely pace at which it would reduce the statutory tax rate by 3 percent on average. However, the U.S. tax reform lowered the corporate rate by 12 percent and this forced Canada to accelerate its own reforms. The danger was that Canada would lose tax revenue to the U.S. because multinationals would report their revenue in the U.S. and their costs in Canada.

In 1987 the Canadian system reduced many exemptions and reduced tax rates to the following levels: 28 percent for large non-manufacturing firms, 23 percent for large manufacturing firms, and 12 percent for small firms. This provided the federal government with roughly $5 billion in extra revenue between 1988 and 1992. What was supposed to have been a reform to make things more efficient turned out to be a cash cow. Most provinces also levy a corporate tax, though at much lower rates than those from the federal government. Table 7.1 and the accompanying Figure 7.1 show how federal and provincial corporate taxes have varied in the period 1984-1992.

Table 7.1 Provincial and federal corporate tax collections, 1984-1992 (in 1992 dollars)

Year	Provincial	Federal	Total
	Millions of Dollars (1992=100)		
1984	6,325	12,972	19,297
1986	6,916	12,633	19,549
1987	7,910	13,316	21,227
1988	8,794	13,804	22,598
1989	9,412	14,237	23,649
1990	9,260	13,261	22,521
1991	6,715	8,506	15,222
1992	7,340	9,500	16,840

Source: Federal and provincial budgets and public accounts.

Why is it so popular?

The corporate tax has great political appeal for two reasons. It is deeply engrained in public opinion that corporations are agglomerations of wealthy stockholders who can always "afford" to be squeezed a little harder. Surprisingly, it is also a popular tax with many corporations on the margins of profitability. Corporations with no profits pay no corporate tax. Other types of tax such as business property levies are widely disliked because they can put a company in the red. The corporate tax can never do this.

Figure 7.1:
Provincial and Federal Corporate Tax Collections, 1984-1992
(millions of 1992 dollars)

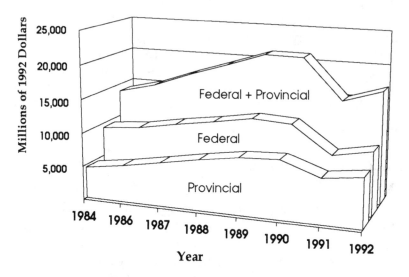

Should it be so popular?

Corporations are, of course, not the preserve of a wealthy few. When ordinary working people entrust their savings to a mutual fund manager, that money is invested in corporations and the income of those corporations flows back to these small investors. Money set aside by employers for pensions is also invested in corporations through this roundabout method.

What is less obvious, but equally true, is that homeowners, farmers, cab drivers and anyone who owns capital in the non-corporate sector of the economy also feels the impact of taxes on the corporate sector. How can this be? The reason lies in that capital is very mobile. If the opportunities for making money in the corporate sector are reduced, investors will look for opportunities abroad, and at home in the non-corporate sector. This sector is largely made up of agriculture, real estate. As investors transfer their corporate capital to this sector, capital will become more abundant there, and the returns to capital there will fall. For example, investors in high technology stocks may find the corporate tax gives them too little return and they may decide to invest their money in an egg farm. This will add to the number of egg farms, increase the number of eggs produced and lower the margins of profit for egg farmers. Thus, the tax in the corporate high-tech sector also is, in effect, a tax on the non-corporate, egg sector.

This is one of many possible examples that show why measuring who pays the corporate tax is a tricky question. It is also possible that companies will pass it on in the form of higher prices, or that capital will simply leave the country, thereby making labour less productive and reducing wages.

Estimating the Canadian corporate tax

Since none of these assumptions can be dismissed offhand, there is bound to be controversy over any single estimate of who bears the corporate tax. This is why it is customary to make several sets of calculations, each based on different, but plausible assumptions. The main assumption we use in our calculations is that owners of capital in both the corporate and non-corporate sectors bear the corporate tax, but for balance we show what most of our results would look like if labour bore the entire tax or if it were passed on entirely to consumers.

Table 7.2 and Figure 7.2 show the breakdown of the corporate tax by lower, middle, and upper income groups.[13] As expected, the upper income group bears most of this tax. Since the late 1980s this group's burden has grown, perhaps because of the disappearance of many corporate tax breaks after the reforms of 1987. Income deciles, however, do not tell us anything about the personal characteristics of taxpayers. A relevant question is how much of the tax various age groups pay. Are the elderly inconvenienced? Or do the young and middle-aged bear the

---

13   The lower income group comprises of people in the bottom three deciles. The middle contains the middle four deciles, and the upper income group contains the top three income deciles.

Table 7.2: Decile distribution of profit taxes

Year	Lower Income Groups	Middle Income Groups	Upper Income Groups
1976	10.30	17.80	71.90
1981	12.20	31.80	56.00
1984	10.99	35.33	53.68
1987	11.64	36.82	51.55
1992	5.52	27.48	67.00

Figure 7.2:
What Percentage of the Corporate Tax Each
Income Group Paid, 1976-1992

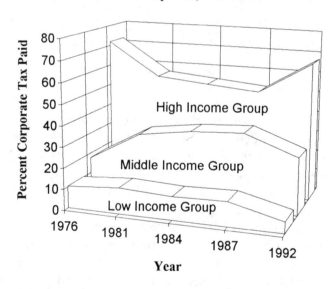

greater part? Table 7.3 and Figure 7.3 show how much of all taxes that the government collects are paid by people of different age groups, and compares this to how much corporate tax each age group pays. Even though people above 65 pay little tax overall, they bear a disproportionate amount of the corporate tax.

Table 7.3: Total tax and total corporate tax paid by age group, 1992

Age Group	Corporate Tax (millions of dollars)	Share of Corporate Tax Paid by Age Group	Total Tax (millions of dollars)
16 ≤ Age < 24	$ 131	0.80%	$ 4,503
24 ≤ Age < 32	452	2.76	32,540
32 ≤ Age < 40	950	5.81	47,980
40 ≤ Age < 48	1,330	8.13	50,642
48 ≤ Age < 56	1,631	9.97	36,519
56 ≤ Age < 64	3,412	20.87	33,017
64 ≤ Age < 72	4,321	26.43	21,928
72 ≤ Age < 80	2,960	18.10	12,641
80 ≤ Age	1,162	7.11	4,783

Source: Fraser Institute Canadian Tax Simulator (CANTASIM).

These results are not surprising under our assumption that capital bears the tax. The elderly and retired receive most of their income from capital sources such as retirement funds and rental property. A "sensitivity" analysis here can alert us to some different tax-bearing scenarios. Figure 7.4 shows how much different age groups would pay under the assumptions that 1) Capital bears the entire tax 2) Capital and labour share the burden equally[14] 3) Labour bears the entire burden. As we can see, the results are very different depending on which assumptions we make. How reasonable each assumption is depends on what we believe about the mobility of capital between the corporate and non-corporate sectors, and between Canada and the rest of the world. The more mobile

---

14 That is to say, capital and labour bear the tax in proportion to their shares in national income.

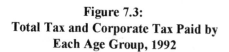

Figure 7.3:
Total Tax and Corporate Tax Paid by
Each Age Group, 1992

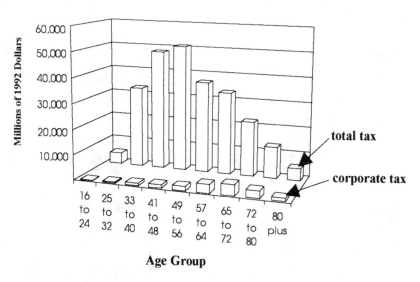

capital is, the less of the burden of the tax it will bear. There is an active debate over the degree to which capital can pass the tax on to labour—a debate which we cannot resolve here. The point to keep in mind is that it is *people* who pay the corporate tax. Under two of three possible scenarios (capital bears all, or capital and labour bear equally) the elderly pay significantly for a policy which is widely but misleadingly touted as a tax on the profits of corporations.

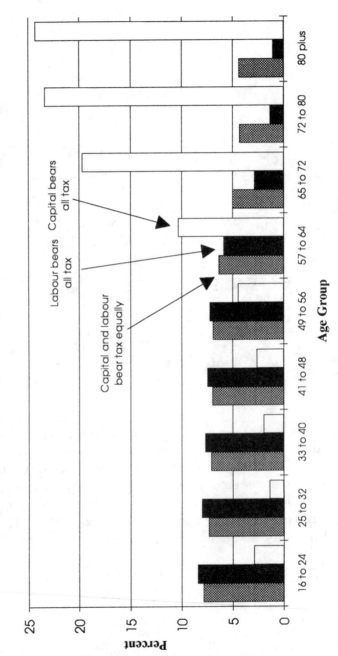

Figure 7.4:
Corporate Taxes as a Percentage of Average Taxes Paid within Each Age Group, 1992

Appendix

How to Calculate Your Tax Rates

THIS APPENDIX IS A SIMPLE TOOL for letting you discover how much tax you really pay. There are four sets of tables for each province and for Canada as a whole, and it is up to you to decide which is most relevant. Suppose your most significant feature is that you are above 65 and have a family income of $35,000 anually. Turn to table A-1 for your province and scan how much tax someone in your age and income bracket pays. This is your answer. Other dimensions are also provided. Table A-2 shows how much tax families pay by gender of head and by income level. Table A-3 divides tax by families above and below Statistics Canada's low income cut-offs, or LICO (base = 1986). Table A-4 compares taxes paid with family size.

Appendix Table A-1: Average tax bill of families with head under 65 years of age, and 65 years or older, by income group for Canada and the provinces, 1992 (dollars)

CANADA

Income Group		Under 65	65 or older
Under $10,000	Average Tax	$813	$828
	Standard Deviation	1,075	1,475
$10,000–$15,000	Average Tax	2,855	924
	Standard Deviation	2,262	1,356
$15,000–$20,000	Average Tax	5,099	946
	Standard Deviation	2,845	2,130
$20,000–$25,000	Average Tax	8,023	1,965
	Standard Deviation	3,315	2,527
$25,000–$30,000	Average Tax	10,435	6,107
	Standard Deviation	3,608	4,443
$30,000–$35,000	Average Tax	12,967	5,438
	Standard Deviation	4,120	5,657
$35,000–$40,000	Average Tax	15,322	9,661
	Standard Deviation	4,379	6,592
$40,000–$45,000	Average Tax	18,587	13,869
	Standard Deviation	4,927	6,640
$45,000–$50,000	Average Tax	20,895	18,061
	Standard Deviation	5,093	7,589
$50,000–$55,000	Average Tax	23,921	21,270
	Standard Deviation	5,306	7,474
$55,000–$60,000	Average Tax	26,351	23,612
	Standard Deviation	5,689	7,592
$60,000–$65,000	Average Tax	28,913	27,084
	Standard Deviation	6,611	7,825
$65,000–$70,000	Average Tax	31,287	32,595
	Standard Deviation	7,059	9,113

$70,000–$75,000	Average Tax	34,381	35,831
	Standard Deviation	8,052	8,982
$75,000–$80,000	Average Tax	36,684	36,791
	Standard Deviation	7,475	10,054
$80,000–$90,000	Average Tax	40,912	42,678
	Standard Deviation	8,956	11,488
$90,000–$100,000	Average Tax	45,609	4,9319
	Standard Deviation	9,949	12,913
$100,000 and over	Average Tax	70,157	90,573
	Standard Deviation	30,755	54,287
Column Total	Average Tax	25,368	18,790
	Standard Deviation	23,002	29,401

NEWFOUNDLAND

Income Group		Under 65	65 or older
Under $10,000	Average Tax	$1,339	—
	Standard Deviation	1,705	—
$10,000–$15,000	Average Tax	1,688	195
	Standard Deviation	1,799	296
$15,000–$20,000	Average Tax	43,11	14
	Standard Deviation	3,584	1
$20,000–$25,000	Average Tax	6,287	222
	Standard Deviation	4,291	644
$25,000–$30,000	Average Tax	8,821	1,656
	Standard Deviation	4,741	2,893
$30,000–$35,000	Average Tax	10,229	3,951
	Standard Deviation	5,893	4,634
$35,000–$40,000	Average Tax	13,027	3,292
	Standard Deviation	5,426	4,884
$40,000–$45,000	Average Tax	15,914	3,793
	Standard Deviation	6,884	4,485
$45,000–$50,000	Average Tax	19,773	9,038
	Standard Deviation	6,339	7,112
$50,000–$55,000	Average Tax	24,448	11,563
	Standard Deviation	7,847	6,958
$55,000–$60,000	Average Tax	26,180	14,163
	Standard Deviation	8,385	8,065
$60,000–$65,000	Average Tax	29,329	20,090
	Standard Deviation	9,541	12,721
$65,000–$70,000	Average Tax	30,257	17,161
	Standard Deviation	11,764	12,438
$70,000–$75,000	Average Tax	33,762	16,600
	Standard Deviation	10,990	9,707
$75,000–$80,000	Average Tax	34,354	20,132
	Standard Deviation	13,469	6,216
$80,000–$90,000	Average Tax	39,504	25,914
	Standard Deviation	11,647	6,549
$90,000–$100,000	Average Tax	48,263	38,820
	Standard Deviation	11,419	10,370
$100,000 and over	Average Tax	69,655	58,077
	Standard Deviation	32,888	23,435
Column Total	Average Tax	20,194	8,899
	Standard Deviation	18,562	14,040

PRINCE EDWARD ISLAND

Income Group		Under 65	65 or older
Under $10,000	Average Tax	$909	$ —
	Standard Deviation	1,055	—
$10,000–$15,000	Average Tax	2,766	181
	Standard Deviation	2,491	154
$15,000–$20,000	Average Tax	5,186	144
	Standard Deviation	2,879	338
$20,000–$25,000	Average Tax	8,564	2,204
	Standard Deviation	2,922	1,682
$25,000–$30,000	Average Tax	9,457	6,050
	Standard Deviation	3,279	4,876
$30,000–$35,000	Average Tax	11,577	3,045
	Standard Deviation	3,818	3,860
$35,000–$40,000	Average Tax	13,755	10,413
	Standard Deviation	3,411	5,953
$40,000–$45,000	Average Tax	16,822	9,761
	Standard Deviation	3,699	5,962
$45,000–$50,000	Average Tax	20,359	14,811
	Standard Deviation	3,925	5,421
$50,000–$55,000	Average Tax	22,779	16,756
	Standard Deviation	4,275	4,149
$55,000–$60,000	Average Tax	26360	18,854
	Standard Deviation	5,000	3,392
$60,000–$65,000	Average Tax	29,228	23,212
	Standard Deviation	4,685	9,059
$65,000–$70,000	Average Tax	30,789	17,776
	Standard Deviation	5,839	1,946
$70,000–$75,000	Average Tax	29,821	37,479
	Standard Deviation	7,597	5,467
$75,000–$80,000	Average Tax	31,307	45,032
	Standard Deviation	7,961	—
$80,000–$90,000	Average Tax	34,846	41,362
	Standard Deviation	7,874	—
$90,000–$100,000	Average Tax	41,259	27,580
	Standard Deviation	9,588	—
$100,000 and over	Average Tax	72,487	102,710
	Standard Deviation	3,3096	106,929
Column Total	Average Tax	17,082	9,482
	Standard Deviation	17,115	27,429

NOVA SCOTIA

Income Group		Under 65	65 or older
Under $10,000	Average Tax	$890	$346
	Standard Deviation	1,067	280
$10,000–$15,000	Average Tax	2,631	720
	Standard Deviation	1,879	1465
$15,000–$20,000	Average Tax	5,666	729
	Standard Deviation	2,451	1,152
$20,000–$25,000	Average Tax	7,836	2,875
	Standard Deviation	2,865	2,333
$25,000–$30,000	Average Tax	10,242	2,524
	Standard Deviation	2,876	3,499
$30,000–$35,000	Average Tax	12,966	5,843
	Standard Deviation	3,194	3,798
$35,000–$40,000	Average Tax	16,310	9,917
	Standard Deviation	3,051	3,210
$40,000–$45,000	Average Tax	19,147	10,680
	Standard Deviation	3,435	5,474
$45,000–$50,000	Average Tax	20,805	17,888
	Standard Deviation	3,917	6,327
$50,000–$55,000	Average Tax	23,753	19,551
	Standard Deviation	4,958	6,446
$55,000–$60,000	Average Tax	27,084	19,539
	Standard Deviation	6,316	7,653
$60,000–$65,000	Average Tax	29,649	22,456
	Standard Deviation	6,922	4,351
$65,000–$70,000	Average Tax	31,895	23,431
	Standard Deviation	5,188	6,783
$70,000–$75,000	Average Tax	34,748	30,904
	Standard Deviation	6,247	7,535
$75,000–$80,000	Average Tax	38,819	38,512
	Standard Deviation	8,031	9,398
$80,000–$90,000	Average Tax	40,812	32,369
	Standard Deviation	8,327	3,315
$90,000–$100,000	Average Tax	46,353	40,336
	Standard Deviation	8,943	1,1778
$100,000 and over	Average Tax	66,960	75,094
	Standard Deviation	22,227	44,251
Column Total	Average Tax	19,771	10,408
	Standard Deviation	17,744	19,229

NEW BRUNSWICK

Income Group		Under 65	65 or older
Under $10,000	Average Tax	$665	$14
	Standard Deviation	837	—
$10,000–$15,000	Average Tax	2,215	1,158
	Standard Deviation	2,137	977
$15,000–$20,000	Average Tax	4,600	305
	Standard Deviation	2,979	739
$20,000–$25,000	Average Tax	7,458	2,242
	Standard Deviation	3,112	2,275
$25,000–$30,000	Average Tax	9,821	5,144
	Standard Deviation	3,324	3,403
$30,000–$35,000	Average Tax	12,342	2,360
	Standard Deviation	3,852	3,601
$35,000–$40,000	Average Tax	15,049	5,731
	Standard Deviation	3,623	4,137
$40,000–$45,000	Average Tax	18,035	8,876
	Standard Deviation	4,323	4,900
$45,000–$50,000	Average Tax	20,652	12,016
	Standard Deviation	4,288	5,248
$50,000–$55,000	Average Tax	23,285	14,600
	Standard Deviation	4,730	8,238
$55,000–$60,000	Average Tax	27,112	19,906
	Standard Deviation	4,846	5,847
$60,000–$65,000	Average Tax	28,101	21,347
	Standard Deviation	7,297	9,220
$65,000–$70,000	Average Tax	31,769	27,561
	Standard Deviation	6,856	8,520
$70,000–$75,000	Average Tax	33,390	31,283
	Standard Deviation	6,566	7,106
$75,000–$80,000	Average Tax	35,376	30,226
	Standard Deviation	8,185	14,503
$80,000–$90,000	Average Tax	39,433	35,104
	Standard Deviation	8,976	8,525
$90,000–$100,000	Average Tax	45,968	39,859
	Standard Deviation	9,333	6,710
$100,000 and over	Average Tax	64,989	63,429
	Standard Deviation	35,325	21,519
Column Total	Average Tax	19,918	11,503
	Standard Deviation	18,713	16,628

QUEBEC

Income Group		Under 65	65 or older
Under $10,000	Average Tax	$656	$166
	Standard Deviation	1,062	573
$10,000–$15,000	Average Tax	2,765	560
	Standard Deviation	2,467	1,390
$15,000–$20,000	Average Tax	5,344	636
	Standard Deviation	3,028	1,505
$20,000–$25,000	Average Tax	8,837	913
	Standard Deviation	3,226	1,531
$25,000–$30,000	Average Tax	11,159	4,518
	Standard Deviation	3,884	3,898
$30,000–$35,000	Average Tax	13,719	3,716
	Standard Deviation	4,333	4,301
$35,000–$40,000	Average Tax	16,443	7,937
	Standard Deviation	4,809	5,900
$40,000–$45,000	Average Tax	20,322	11,695
	Standard Deviation	5,182	5,268
$45,000–$50,000	Average Tax	22,239	15,983
	Standard Deviation	4,716	6,196
$50,000–$55,000	Average Tax	25,924	19,435
	Standard Deviation	5,021	6,327
$55,000–$60,000	Average Tax	29,840	21,758
	Standard Deviation	4,843	5,515
$60,000–$65,000	Average Tax	31,671	23,140
	Standard Deviation	6,133	6,615
$65,000–$70,000	Average Tax	34,428	30,458
	Standard Deviation	7,372	7,852
$70,000–$75,000	Average Tax	37,494	37,061
	Standard Deviation	7,847	10,130
$75,000–$80,000	Average Tax	40,612	33,424
	Standard Deviation	7,704	7,323
$80,000–$90,000	Average Tax	44,796	37,382
	Standard Deviation	9,744	8,850
$90,000–$100,000	Average Tax	52,137	45,783
	Standard Deviation	9,066	7,336
$100,000 and over	Average Tax	78,843	86,402
	Standard Deviation	39,052	62,210
Column Total	Average Tax	23,845	12,526
	Standard Deviation	22,484	23,852

ONTARIO

Income Group		Under 65	65 or older
Under $10,000	Average Tax	$898	$1,204
	Standard Deviation	1158	1,350
$10,000–$15,000	Average Tax	3,193	1,389
	Standard Deviation	2,268	1,380
$15,000–$20,000	Average Tax	4,923	1,085
	Standard Deviation	2,745	2,125
$20,000–$25,000	Average Tax	7,696	2,789
	Standard Deviation	3,207	2,908
$25,000–$30,000	Average Tax	10,534	7,482
	Standard Deviation	3,141	4,377
$30,000–$35,000	Average Tax	13,052	6,635
	Standard Deviation	3,583	6,058
$35,000–$40,000	Average Tax	15,197	12,618
	Standard Deviation	4,107	6,257
$40,000–$45,000	Average Tax	18,731	17,012
	Standard Deviation	4,722	5,102
$45,000–$50,000	Average Tax	20,521	19,382
	Standard Deviation	4,655	7,168
$50,000–$55,000	Average Tax	23,361	22,910
	Standard Deviation	4,776	6,427
$55,000–$60,000	Average Tax	24,954	25,433
	Standard Deviation	5,075	7,715
$60,000–$65,000	Average Tax	28,233	27,719
	Standard Deviation	6,096	7,187
$65,000–$70,000	Average Tax	30,445	35,129
	Standard Deviation	5,531	6,421
$70,000–$75,000	Average Tax	34,134	36,609
	Standard Deviation	7,438	6,951
$75,000–$80,000	Average Tax	35,599	389,22
	Standard Deviation	5,715	9,451
$80,000–$90,000	Average Tax	40,394	43,116
	Standard Deviation	7,997	10,656
$90,000–$100,000	Average Tax	43,151	51,734
	Standard Deviation	9,160	10,306
$100,000 and over	Average Tax	69,037	93,936
	Standard Deviation	27,164	58,543
Column Total	Average Tax	29,404	23,535
	Standard Deviation	24,522	33,294

MANITOBA

Income Group		Under 65	65 or older
Under $10,000	Average Tax	$801	$7
	Standard Deviation	807	1
$10,000–$15,000	Average Tax	3,093	102
	Standard Deviation	2,058	217
$15,000–$20,000	Average Tax	4,880	1,068
	Standard Deviation	2,346	2,203
$20,000–$25,000	Average Tax	7,742	2,741
	Standard Deviation	2,899	2,436
$25,000–$30,000	Average Tax	9,612	6,352
	Standard Deviation	3,262	3,489
$30,000–$35,000	Average Tax	12,588	6,888
	Standard Deviation	4,179	6,470
$35,000–$40,000	Average Tax	14,437	10,540
	Standard Deviation	3,910	6,043
$40,000–$45,000	Average Tax	16,165	16,099
	Standard Deviation	4435	5,181
$45,000–$50,000	Average Tax	20,767	19,083
	Standard Deviation	6,603	5,663
$50,000–$55,000	Average Tax	22,548	22,332
	Standard Deviation	5,531	6,057
$55,000–$60,000	Average Tax	25,011	23,096
	Standard Deviation	6,766	6,434
$60,000–$65,000	Average Tax	26,707	26,046
	Standard Deviation	5,749	7,186
$65,000–$70,000	Average Tax	29,252	36,842
	Standard Deviation	7,378	7,826
$70,000–$75,000	Average Tax	32,334	28,408
	Standard Deviation	7,685	10,309
$75,000–$80,000	Average Tax	33,719	36,867
	Standard Deviation	8,579	5,069
$80,000–$90,000	Average Tax	38,619	38,897
	Standard Deviation	9,534	8,807
$90,000–$100,000	Average Tax	45,911	33,949
	Standard Deviation	8,621	11,680
$100,000 and over	Average Tax	67,526	74,549
	Standard Deviation	33,979	29,882
Column Total	Average Tax	22,288	15,514
	Standard Deviation	21,937	19,352

SASKATCHEWAN

Income Group		Under 65	65 or older
Under $10,000	Average Tax	$1,001	$598
	Standard Deviation	1,153	694
$10,000–$15,000	Average Tax	3,132	5,245
	Standard Deviation	2,039	—
$15,000–$20,000	Average Tax	5,161	1,946
	Standard Deviation	2,972	3,540
$20,000–$25,000	Average Tax	7,614	2,088
	Standard Deviation	2,971	2,299
$25,000–$30,000	Average Tax	10,081	7,543
	Standard Deviation	39,23	4,477
$30,000–$35,000	Average Tax	12,491	6,562
	Standard Deviation	3,773	6,555
$35,000–$40,000	Average Tax	14,939	8,351
	Standard Deviation	4,280	5,935
$40,000–$45,000	Average Tax	17,405	15,123
	Standard Deviation	4,384	6,550
$45,000–$50,000	Average Tax	21,032	17,380
	Standard Deviation	5,511	7,335
$50,000–$55,000	Average Tax	23,208	22,085
	Standard Deviation	5,499	7,486
$55,000–$60,000	Average Tax	27,136	21,213
	Standard Deviation	6,241	7,654
$60,000–$65,000	Average Tax	28,142	28,965
	Standard Deviation	6,654	7,295
$65,000–$70,000	Average Tax	32,149	33,513
	Standard Deviation	7,744	11,359
$70,000–$75,000	Average Tax	35,288	45,305
	Standard Deviation	6,793	9,440
$75,000–$80,000	Average Tax	38,687	40,132
	Standard Deviation	8,902	14,727
$80,000–$90,000	Average Tax	42,508	50,135
	Standard Deviation	12,168	14,079
$90,000–$100,000	Average Tax	46,975	59,243
	Standard Deviation	11,084	18,324
$100,000 and over	Average Tax	68,117	97521
	Standard Deviation	26,954	47,752
Column Total	Average Tax	22,194	18,766
	Standard Deviation	20,630	28,241

ALBERTA

Income Group		Under 65	65 or older
Under $10,000	Average Tax	$823	$1,135
	Standard Deviation	913	1,741
$10,000–$15,000	Average Tax	2,603	66
	Standard Deviation	2,197	110
$15,000–$20,000	Average Tax	4,440	5,714
	Standard Deviation	2,793	7,196
$20,000–$25,000	Average Tax	6,450	1,621
	Standard Deviation	3,257	2,774
$25,000–$30,000	Average Tax	9,043	6,579
	Standard Deviation	3,669	4,418
$30,000–$35,000	Average Tax	1,1472	8,180
	Standard Deviation	4,666	6,765
$35,000–$40,000	Average Tax	13,221	7,852
	Standard Deviation	4,453	8,236
$40,000–$45,000	Average Tax	16,107	13,096
	Standard Deviation	4,553	8,752
$45,000–$50,000	Average Tax	18,253	16,548
	Standard Deviation	4,934	8,979
$50,000–$55,000	Average Tax	20,711	22,210
	Standard Deviation	5,105	10,296
$55,000–$60,000	Average Tax	23,820	24,520
	Standard Deviation	5,501	12,108
$60,000–$65,000	Average Tax	26,159	30,064
	Standard Deviation	7,872	10,075
$65,000–$70,000	Average Tax	27,978	37,437
	Standard Deviation	7,038	12,365
$70,000–$75,000	Average Tax	30,419	39,148
	Standard Deviation	9,355	13,265
$75,000–$80,000	Average Tax	32,999	38,179
	Standard Deviation	7,566	11,524
$80,000–$90,000	Average Tax	37,571	53,251
	Standard Deviation	8,266	17,062
$90,000–$100,000	Average Tax	42,016	67,935
	Standard Deviation	9,234	18,795
$100,000 and over	Average Tax	68,041	109,222
	Standard Deviation	34,152	57,578
Column Total	Average Tax	22,948	25,069
	Standard Deviation	23,093	39,103

BRITISH COLUMBIA

Income Group		Under 65	65 or older
Under $10,000	Average Tax	$918	$4,132
	Standard Deviation	1,020	3,804
$10,000–$15,000	Average Tax	2,741	782
	Standard Deviation	1,929	526
$15,000–$20,000	Average Tax	5,476	760
	Standard Deviation	2,564	1,483
$20,000–$25,000	Average Tax	8,644	2,762
	Standard Deviation	3,284	2,768
$25,000–$30,000	Average Tax	10,542	7,199
	Standard Deviation	3,323	4,318
$30,000–$35,000	Average Tax	12,875	5,589
	Standard Deviation	3,630	5,747
$35,000–$40,000	Average Tax	15,279	10,762
	Standard Deviation	3,609	5,699
$40,000–$45,000	Average Tax	17,642	13,810
	Standard Deviation	3,425	6,474
$45,000–$50,000	Average Tax	20,792	20,015
	Standard Deviation	5,741	8,405
$50,000–$55,000	Average Tax	24,008	22,852
	Standard Deviation	5,298	7,213
$55,000–$60,000	Average Tax	25,568	26,238
	Standard Deviation	4,764	6,203
$60,000–$65,000	Average Tax	27,523	29,878
	Standard Deviation	5,788	6,773
$65,000–$70,000	Average Tax	30,055	31,933
	Standard Deviation	7,127	3,855
$70,000–$75,000	Average Tax	33,016	34,400
	Standard Deviation	7,636	7,489
$75,000–$80,000	Average Tax	35,902	39,652
	Standard Deviation	6,825	9,094
$80,000–$90,000	Average Tax	38,886	44,959
	Standard Deviation	7,050	5,649
$90,000–$100,000	Average Tax	46,699	42,681
	Standard Deviation	9,677	9,191
$100,000and over	Average Tax	67,593	81,573
	Standard Deviation	29,146	33,559
Column Total	Average Tax	24,199	21,150
	Standard Deviation	21,218	27,290

Appendix Table A–2: Average tax bill of families by gender of head of the family and by income group for Canada and the provinces (dollars)

CANADA

Income Group		Male head	Female head
Under $10,000	Average Tax	$800	$826
	Standard Deviation	1,044	1,127
$10,000–$15,000	Average Tax	2,895	2,688
	Standard Deviation	2,211	2,307
$15,000–$20,000	Average Tax	4,189	3,735
	Standard Deviation	3,009	3,463
$20,000–$25,000	Average Tax	6,548	4,269
	Standard Deviation	4,012	4,144
$25,000–$30,000	Average Tax	8,781	10,144
	Standard Deviation	4,375	4,002
$30,000–$35,000	Average Tax	9,889	13,247
	Standard Deviation	5,890	4,558
$35,000–$40,000	Average Tax	13,362	16,214
	Standard Deviation	5,542	4,929
$40,000–$45,000	Average Tax	17,340	19,253
	Standard Deviation	5,529	5,623
$45,000–$50,000	Average Tax	20,118	21,908
	Standard Deviation	5,594	5,905
$50,000–$55,000	Average Tax	23,297	25,029
	Standard Deviation	5,636	5,997
$55,000–$60,000	Average Tax	25,808	27,639
	Standard Deviation	5,862	7,237
$60,000–$65,000	Average Tax	28,511	29,959
	Standard Deviation	6,698	7,803
$65,000–$70,000	Average Tax	31,268	33,020
	Standard Deviation	7,279	7,476

$70,000–$75,000	Average Tax	34,470	35,938
	Standard Deviation	8,057	9,659
$75,000–$80,000	Average Tax	36,513	39,323
	Standard Deviation	7,669	9,431
$80,000–$90,000	Average Tax	40,865	44,059
	Standard Deviation	8,824	13,351
$90,000–$100,000	Average Tax	45,947	47,550
	Standard Deviation	10,153	13,687
$100,000 and over	Average Tax	72,541	83,930
	Standard Deviation	35,061	47,319
Column Total	Average Tax	27,872	12,351
	Standard Deviation	25,336	16,731

NEWFOUNDLAND

Income Group		Male head	Female head
Under $10,000	Average Tax	$1,876	$1,007
	Standard Deviation	2,115	1,286
$10,000–$15,000	Average Tax	1,840	1,288
	Standard Deviation	1,909	1,548
$15,000–$20,000	Average Tax	3,884	4,622
	Standard Deviation	3,041	4,564
$20,000–$25,000	Average Tax	4,639	4,286
	Standard Deviation	4,324	4,759
$25,000–$30,000	Average Tax	7,495	6,371
	Standard Deviation	5,021	5,991
$30,000–$35,000	Average Tax	9,233	8,358
	Standard Deviation	5,873	7,081
$35,000–$40,000	Average Tax	9,682	14,014
	Standard Deviation	6,400	8,572
$40,000–$45,000	Average Tax	12,939	17,192
	Standard Deviation	8,119	7,606
$45,000–$50,000	Average Tax	18,103	16,263
	Standard Deviation	7,630	7,565
$50,000–$55,000	Average Tax	22,359	22,227
	Standard Deviation	8,981	9,585
$55,000–$60,000	Average Tax	24,917	22,361
	Standard Deviation	9,200	9,068
$60,000–$65,000	Average Tax	28,134	27,973
	Standard Deviation	9,900	14,148
$65,000–$70,000	Average Tax	27,382	29,338
	Standard Deviation	12,568	15,626
$70,000–$75,000	Average Tax	31,726	19,845
	Standard Deviation	12,371	5,243
$75,000–$80,000	Average Tax	33,598	17,079
	Standard Deviation	13,451	6,206
$80,000–$90,000	Average Tax	38,281	30,853
	Standard Deviation	12,216	5,730
$90,000–$100,000	Average Tax	47,919	38,448
	Standard Deviation	11,907	4,079
$100,000 and over	Average Tax	68,611	56,986
	Standard Deviation	32,574	11,983
Column Total	Average Tax	20,092	10,070
	Standard Deviation	19,049	12,063

PRINCE EDWARD ISLAND

Income Group		Male Head	Female Head
Under $10,000	Average Tax	$1,274	$655
	Standard Deviation	1,200	853
$10,000–$15,000	Average Tax	2,422	2,875
	Standard Deviation	2,210	2,687
$15,000–$20,000	Average Tax	3,126	2,643
	Standard Deviation	2,741	3,667
$20,000–$25,000	Average Tax	7,325	7,023
	Standard Deviation	3,086	4,399
$25,000–$30,000	Average Tax	8,205	10,148
	Standard Deviation	4,098	2,937
$30,000–$35,000	Average Tax	7,493	10,023
	Standard Deviation	5,766	4,806
$35,000–$40,000	Average Tax	13,619	9,441
	Standard Deviation	4,221	3,116
$40,000–$45,000	Average Tax	15,447	12,269
	Standard Deviation	5,112	5,693
$45,000–$50,000	Average Tax	19,275	18,462
	Standard Deviation	4,756	5,400
$50,000–$55,000	Average Tax	22,406	13,885
	Standard Deviation	4,459	2,799
$55,000–$60,000	Average Tax	26,071	20,093
	Standard Deviation	5,188	3,807
$60,000–$65,000	Average Tax	28,853	24,760
	Standard Deviation	5,498	7,508
$65,000–$70,000	Average Tax	29,829	—
	Standard Deviation	6,590	—
$70,000–$75,000	Average Tax	30,630	—
	Standard Deviation	7,765	—
$75,000–$80,000	Average Tax	32,045	—
	Standard Deviation	8,341	—
$80,000–$90,000	Average Tax	35,297	35,422
	Standard Deviation	7,933	—
$90,000–$100,000	Average Tax	37,160	52,290
	Standard Deviation	8,613	1,429
$100,000 and over	Average Tax	77,641	94,068
	Standard Deviation	56,786	—
Column Total	Average Tax	18,291	6,909
	Standard Deviation	21,718	9,947

NOVA SCOTIA

Income Group		Male Head	Female Head
Under $10,000	Average Tax	$956	$824
	Standard Deviation	1,204	921
$10,000–$15,000	Average Tax	2,764	2,164
	Standard Deviation	1,852	1,953
$15,000–$20,000	Average Tax	3,685	2,697
	Standard Deviation	2,893	3,185
$20,000–$25,000	Average Tax	6,087	5,883
	Standard Deviation	3,645	3,520
$25,000–$30,000	Average Tax	7,061	9,746
	Standard Deviation	4,815	4,066
$30,000–$35,000	Average Tax	11,195	10,447
	Standard Deviation	4,505	5,008
$35,000–$40,000	Average Tax	15,090	14,711
	Standard Deviation	3,943	4,318
$40,000–$45,000	Average Tax	17,846	17,862
	Standard Deviation	4,910	4,773
$45,000–$50,000	Average Tax	20,290	21,779
	Standard Deviation	4,498	3,721
$50,000–$55,000	Average Tax	23,029	24,790
	Standard Deviation	5,456	4,405
$55,000–$60,000	Average Tax	25,449	29,596
	Standard Deviation	6,259	11,602
$60,000–$65,000	Average Tax	28,782	29,081
	Standard Deviation	7,157	5,893
$65,000–$70,000	Average Tax	30,918	29,551
	Standard Deviation	6,053	6,632
$70,000–$75,000	Average Tax	34,300	32,672
	Standard Deviation	6,671	5,920
$75,000–$80,000	Average Tax	38,793	—
	Standard Deviation	8,154	—
$80,000–$90,000	Average Tax	40,647	37,969
	Standard Deviation	8,475	6,885
$90,000–$100,000	Average Tax	46,185	34,380
	Standard Deviation	8,764	14,681
$100,000 and over	Average Tax	68,357	70,126
	Standard Deviation	27,808	27,714
Column Total	Average Tax	21,040	8,053
	Standard Deviation	19,196	11,806

NEW BRUNSWICK

Income Group		Male Head	Female Head
Under $10,000	Average Tax	$581	$733
	Standard Deviation	656	961
$10,000–$15,000	Average Tax	2,138	2,239
	Standard Deviation	2,088	2,156
$15,000–$20,000	Average Tax	3,414	2,479
	Standard Deviation	3,273	2,999
$20,000–$25,000	Average Tax	6,422	4,188
	Standard Deviation	3,499	3,766
$25,000–$30,000	Average Tax	9,279	8,285
	Standard Deviation	3,428	4,437
$30,000–$35,000	Average Tax	8,341	10,866
	Standard Deviation	6,026	5,895
$35,000–$40,000	Average Tax	13,136	13,635
	Standard Deviation	5,051	6,602
$40,000–$45,000	Average Tax	15,984	16,721
	Standard Deviation	5,481	7,292
$45,000–$50,000	Average Tax	18,884	19,470
	Standard Deviation	5,556	6,062
$50,000–$55,000	Average Tax	21,357	21,747
	Standard Deviation	6,584	7,759
$55,000–$60,000	Average Tax	26,339	21,648
	Standard Deviation	5,451	6,334
$60,000–$65,000	Average Tax	26,433	33,942
	Standard Deviation	7,288	8,250
$65,000–$70,000	Average Tax	30,472	37,478
	Standard Deviation	7,298	3,293
$70,000–$75,000	Average Tax	32,764	36,294
	Standard Deviation	6,891	1,849
$75,000–$80,000	Average Tax	34,607	32,185
	Standard Deviation	8,748	15,529
$80,000–$90,000	Average Tax	39,011	39,894
	Standard Deviation	9,199	5,906
$90,000–$100,000	Average Tax	45,549	35,827
	Standard Deviation	9,143	5,036
$100,000 and over	Average Tax	65,207	55,602
	Standard Deviation	33,838	18,231
Column Total	Average Tax	21,040	9,204
	Standard Deviation	19,429	11,984

QUEBEC

Income Group		Male Head	Female Head
Under $10,000	Average Tax	$565	$699
	Standard Deviation	1,030	1,068
$10,000–$15,000	Average Tax	2,763	2,621
	Standard Deviation	2,478	2,458
$15,000–$20,000	Average Tax	4,140	4,462
	Standard Deviation	3,232	3,542
$20,000–$25,000	Average Tax	6,926	3,440
	Standard Deviation	4,434	4,334
$25,000–$30,000	Average Tax	8,957	11,210
	Standard Deviation	4,700	4,457
$30,000–$35,000	Average Tax	10,264	13,615
	Standard Deviation	6,358	4,814
$35,000–$40,000	Average Tax	13,908	17,094
	Standard Deviation	6,158	5,906
$40,000–$45,000	Average Tax	18,822	19,801
	Standard Deviation	5,785	7,161
$45,000–$50,000	Average Tax	21,472	22,858
	Standard Deviation	5,256	4,924
$50,000–$55,000	Average Tax	25,333	25,106
	Standard Deviation	5,476	5,665
$55,000–$60,000	Average Tax	28,700	28,368
	Standard Deviation	5,541	7,811
$60,000–$65,000	Average Tax	30,992	29,387
	Standard Deviation	6,419	8,588
$65,000–$70,000	Average Tax	34,323	30,833
	Standard Deviation	7,567	5,733
$70,000–$75,000	Average Tax	37,651	35,972
	Standard Deviation	8,064	7,411
$75,000–$80,000	Average Tax	39,645	38,666
	Standard Deviation	8,113	5,560
$80,000–$90,000	Average Tax	43,675	48,385
	Standard Deviation	9,170	17,937
$90,000–$100,000	Average Tax	51,997	36,876
	Standard Deviation	8,396	12,947
$100,000 and over	Average Tax	79,431	85,285
	Standard Deviation	41,249	60,543
Column Total	Average Tax	25,409	10,696
	Standard Deviation	23,784	16,656

ONTARIO

Income Group		Male Head	Female Head
Under $10,000	Average Tax	$883	$936
	Standard Deviation	973	1,308
$10,000–$15,000	Average Tax	3,127	3,108
	Standard Deviation	1,924	2,473
$15,000–$20,000	Average Tax	4,048	3,147
	Standard Deviation	2,984	3,204
$20,000–$25,000	Average Tax	6,613	4,574
	Standard Deviation	3,756	3,827
$25,000–$30,000	Average Tax	9,372	10,036
	Standard Deviation	4,062	3,396
$30,000–$35,000	Average Tax	10,024	13,494
	Standard Deviation	5,601	3,933
$35,000–$40,000	Average Tax	14,165	15,917
	Standard Deviation	4,803	4,320
$40,000–$45,000	Average Tax	17,842	19,864
	Standard Deviation	4,946	4,243
$45,000–$50,000	Average Tax	19,585	22,576
	Standard Deviation	5,145	5,147
$50,000–$55,000	Average Tax	22,780	25,384
	Standard Deviation	4,849	5,373
$55,000–$60,000	Average Tax	24,552	28,001
	Standard Deviation	5,300	5,449
$60,000–$65,000	Average Tax	27,957	29,817
	Standard Deviation	6,363	5,425
$65,000–$70,000	Average Tax	30,608	33,472
	Standard Deviation	5,672	6,259
$70,000–$75,000	Average Tax	34,421	36,625
	Standard Deviation	7,072	10,311
$75,000–$80,000	Average Tax	35,623	38,938
	Standard Deviation	5,975	8,032
$80,000–$90,000	Average Tax	40,460	43,134
	Standard Deviation	7,978	11,325
$90,000–$100,000	Average Tax	43,945	47,025
	Standard Deviation	9,593	10,662
$100,000 and over	Average Tax	71,440	86,201
	Standard Deviation	32,848	45,531
Column Total	Average Tax	32,601	14,973
	Standard Deviation	27,215	18,642

MANITOBA

Income Group		Male Head	Female Head
Under $10,000	Average Tax	$900	$702
	Standard Deviation	746	843
$10,000–$15,000	Average Tax	2,740	3,357
	Standard Deviation	1,869	2,166
$15,000–$20,000	Average Tax	3,801	3,736
	Standard Deviation	2,669	3,095
$20,000–$25,000	Average Tax	6,915	4,327
	Standard Deviation	3,147	3,656
$25,000–$30,000	Average Tax	8,777	8,273
	Standard Deviation	3,542	3,815
$30,000–$35,000	Average Tax	8,917	14,828
	Standard Deviation	5,945	3,416
$35,000–$40,000	Average Tax	12,809	14,840
	Standard Deviation	4,964	4,821
$40,000–$45,000	Average Tax	15,944	18,177
	Standard Deviation	4,666	3,981
$45,000–$50,000	Average Tax	19,866	23,562
	Standard Deviation	6,334	6,260
$50,000–$55,000	Average Tax	21,889	24,689
	Standard Deviation	5,136	6,664
$55,000–$60,000	Average Tax	24,409	27,539
	Standard Deviation	6,711	6,442
$60,000–$65,000	Average Tax	26,430	29,624
	Standard Deviation	5,933	4,640
$65,000–$70,000	Average Tax	29,730	38,724
	Standard Deviation	7,659	6,350
$70,000–$75,000	Average Tax	31,293	34,268
	Standard Deviation	8,684	3,874
$75,000–$80,000	Average Tax	34,102	34,536
	Standard Deviation	8,519	4,422
$80,000–$90,000	Average Tax	38,457	41,574
	Standard Deviation	9,613	5,293
$90,000–$100,000	Average Tax	44,007	47,237
	Standard Deviation	10,224	1,132
$100,000 and over	Average Tax	67,855	87,586
	Standard Deviation	33,351	33,764
Column Total	Average Tax	24,207	10,471
	Standard Deviation	22,614	13,635

SASKATCHEWAN

Income Group		Male Head	Female Head
Under $10,000	Average Tax	$979	$1003
	Standard Deviation	1,037	1,247
$10,000–$15,000	Average Tax	3,272	3,034
	Standard Deviation	1,788	2,235
$15,000–$20,000	Average Tax	5,143	3,855
	Standard Deviation	3,100	3,385
$20,000–$25,000	Average Tax	5,545	3,677
	Standard Deviation	3,583	3,725
$25,000–$30,000	Average Tax	9,110	10,009
	Standard Deviation	4,356	3,885
$30,000–$35,000	Average Tax	9,003	14,013
	Standard Deviation	5,614	4,402
$35,000–$40,000	Average Tax	11,818	16,782
	Standard Deviation	5,844	3,788
$40,000–$45,000	Average Tax	16,209	20,406
	Standard Deviation	4,763	5,625
$45,000–$50,000	Average Tax	20,098	20,866
	Standard Deviation	5,899	8,194
$50,000–$55,000	Average Tax	22,347	28,183
	Standard Deviation	5,659	6,937
$55,000–$60,000	Average Tax	25,929	31,163
	Standard Deviation	6,168	11,455
$60,000–$65,000	Average Tax	28,143	30,996
	Standard Deviation	6,748	7,187
$65,000–$70,000	Average Tax	32,156	34,563
	Standard Deviation	8,066	10,978
$70,000–$75,000	Average Tax	35,861	46,596
	Standard Deviation	7,106	10,590
$75,000–$80,000	Average Tax	37,567	52,413
	Standard Deviation	8,959	12,132
$80,000–$90,000	Average Tax	42,380	54,786
	Standard Deviation	11,999	13,923
$90,000–$100,000	Average Tax	48,211	91,160
	Standard Deviation	12,218	—
$100,000 and over	Average Tax	72,451	120,439
	Standard Deviation	33,345	33,239
Column Total	Average Tax	24,280	11,728
	Standard Deviation	23,130	18,444

ALBERTA

Income Group		Male Head	Female Head
Under $10,000	Average Tax	$881	$749
	Standard Deviation	1027	747
$10,000–$15,000	Average Tax	3,138	1,989
	Standard Deviation	2,498	1,641
$15,000–$20,000	Average Tax	4,361	4,719
	Standard Deviation	2,459	4,024
$20,000–$25,000	Average Tax	5,560	3,850
	Standard Deviation	3,475	4,001
$25,000–$30,000	Average Tax	7,973	9,162
	Standard Deviation	4,260	3,464
$30,000–$35,000	Average Tax	10,158	12,977
	Standard Deviation	5,180	4,592
$35,000–$40,000	Average Tax	10,484	16,975
	Standard Deviation	5,645	6,023
$40,000–$45,000	Average Tax	14,927	18,008
	Standard Deviation	5,605	6,051
$45,000–$50,000	Average Tax	17,525	20,450
	Standard Deviation	5,029	6,673
$50,000–$55,000	Average Tax	20,657	22,463
	Standard Deviation	5,928	5,837
$55,000–$60,000	Average Tax	23,775	24,748
	Standard Deviation	6,166	7,359
$60,000–$65,000	Average Tax	26,328	29,876
	Standard Deviation	7,611	12,873
$65,000–$70,000	Average Tax	28,385	33,723
	Standard Deviation	7,748	10,315
$70,000–$75,000	Average Tax	31,167	31,825
	Standard Deviation	9,910	12,741
$75,000–$80,000	Average Tax	33,129	38,574
	Standard Deviation	8,125	7,006
$80,000–$90,000	Average Tax	38,891	46,733
	Standard Deviation	9,691	22,480
$90,000–$100,000	Average Tax	43,607	69,873
	Standard Deviation	11,739	22,411
$100,000 and over	Average Tax	73,863	83,740
	Standard Deviation	41,134	42,325
Column Total	Average Tax	26,662	11,231
	Standard Deviation	27,528	14,862

BRITISH COLUMBIA

Income Group		Male Head	Female Head
Under $10,000	Average Tax	$907	$987
	Standard Deviation	1,102	1,123
$10,000–$15,000	Average Tax	2,973	2,376
	Standard Deviation	1,948	1,872
$15,000–$20,000	Average Tax	4,638	4,176
	Standard Deviation	2,806	3,350
$20,000–$25,000	Average Tax	6,814	5,595
	Standard Deviation	4,093	4,251
$25,000–$30,000	Average Tax	8,642	10,581
	Standard Deviation	3,943	3,720
$30,000–$35,000	Average Tax	9,300	13,253
	Standard Deviation	5,786	4,126
$35,000–$40,000	Average Tax	13,405	16,670
	Standard Deviation	4,802	2,971
$40,000–$45,000	Average Tax	16,943	17,847
	Standard Deviation	4,188	4,270
$45,000–$50,000	Average Tax	20,599	20,731
	Standard Deviation	6,257	6,933
$50,000–$55,000	Average Tax	23,510	25,938
	Standard Deviation	5,326	6,711
$55,000–$60,000	Average Tax	25,316	28,490
	Standard Deviation	4,332	8,219
$60,000–$65,000	Average Tax	27,539	31,211
	Standard Deviation	5,726	7,451
$65,000–$70,000	Average Tax	30,084	33,549
	Standard Deviation	6,872	7,776
$70,000–$75,000	Average Tax	33,197	33,270
	Standard Deviation	7,516	9,778
$75,000–$80,000	Average Tax	36,065	51,090
	Standard Deviation	7,014	—
$80,000–$90,000	Average Tax	39,499	41,584
	Standard Deviation	7,048	8,299
$90,000–$100,000	Average Tax	45,389	61,270
	Standard Deviation	9,058	7,509
$100,000 and over	Average Tax	70,645	70,670
	Standard Deviation	30,956	24,308
Column Total	Average Tax	27,322	12,109
	Standard Deviation	23,589	13,952

Appendix Table A–3: Average tax bill of families above and below Statistics Canada's low income cut-offs (LICO) (base=1986) by income group for Canada and the provinces, 1992 (dollars)

CANADA

Income Group		Below LICO	Equal to or above LICO
Under $10,000	Average Tax	$772	$3,630
	Standard Deviation	983	2,807
$10,000–$15,000	Average Tax	2,471	4,258
	Standard Deviation	2,140	2,249
$15,000–$20,000	Average Tax	2,413	5,603
	Standard Deviation	2,725	2,935
$20,000–$25,000	Average Tax	2,538	7,511
	Standard Deviation	3,113	3,697
$25,000–$30,000	Average Tax	5,962	9,974
	Standard Deviation	3,842	4,052
$30,000–$35,000	Average Tax	3,871	11,379
	Standard Deviation	4,788	5,420
$35,000–$40,000	Average Tax	6,548	14,305
	Standard Deviation	5,953	5,292
$40,000–$45,000	Average Tax	5,226	17,842
	Standard Deviation	2,737	5,468
$45,000–$50,000	Average Tax	10,908	20,499
	Standard Deviation	6,885	5,610
$50,000–$55,000	Average Tax	11,515	23,615
	Standard Deviation	4,221	5,671
$55,000–$60,000	Average Tax	10,004	26,035
	Standard Deviation	5,630	5,989
$60,000–$65,000	Average Tax	—	28,652
	Standard Deviation	—	6,827
$65,000–$70,000	Average Tax	—	31,425
	Standard Deviation	—	7,314

$70,000–$75,000	Average Tax	10,503	34,607
	Standard Deviation	—	8,183
$75,000–$80,000	Average Tax	—	36,697
	Standard Deviation	—	7,828
$80,000–$90,000	Average Tax	—	41,127
	Standard Deviation	—	9,319
$90,000–$100,000	Average Tax	—	46,045
	Standard Deviation	—	10,410
$100,000 and over	Average Tax	—	73,037
	Standard Deviation	—	35,759
Column Total	Average Tax	2,331	28,855
	Standard Deviation	3,026	24,519

NEWFOUNDLAND

Income Group		Below LICO	Equal to or above LICO
Under $10,000	Average Tax	$1,213	$7,645
	Standard Deviation	1,469	—
$10,000–$15,000	Average Tax	1,264	4,674
	Standard Deviation	1,426	1,781
$15,000–$20,000	Average Tax	2,408	6,854
	Standard Deviation	3,028	2,669
$20,000–$25,000	Average Tax	1,477	7,468
	Standard Deviation	2,049	4,403
$25,000–$30,000	Average Tax	3,229	8,151
	Standard Deviation	3,201	5,283
$30,000–$35,000	Average Tax	2,878	10,115
	Standard Deviation	3,320	5,937
$35,000–$40,000	Average Tax	1,054	10,707
	Standard Deviation	1,449	6,708
$40,000–$45,000	Average Tax	3,593	13,408
	Standard Deviation	3,233	8,121
$45,000–$50,000	Average Tax	6,436	17,997
	Standard Deviation	—	7,611
$50,000–$55,000	Average Tax	3,967	22,622
	Standard Deviation	—	8,841
$55,000–$60,000	Average Tax	—	24,744
	Standard Deviation	—	9,213
$60,000–$65,000	Average Tax	—	28,115
	Standard Deviation	—	10,491
$65,000–$70,000	Average Tax	—	27,628
	Standard Deviation	—	13,006
$70,000–$75,000	Average Tax	—	31,274
	Standard Deviation	—	12,386
$75,000–$80,000	Average Tax	—	33,007
	Standard Deviation	—	13,610
$80,000–$90,000	Average Tax	—	37,739
	Standard Deviation	—	12,019
$90,000–$100,000	Average Tax	—	47,015
	Standard Deviation	—	11,729
$100,000 and over	Average Tax	—	68,075
	Standard Deviation	—	32,010
Column Total	Average Tax	1,845	21,445
	Standard Deviation	2,415	18,416

PRINCE EDWARD ISLAND

Income Group		Below LICO	Equal to or above LICO
Under $10,000	Average Tax	$909	$ —
	Standard Deviation	1,055	—
$10,000–$15,000	Average Tax	1,020	4,330
	Standard Deviation	1,416	2,225
$15,000–$20,000	Average Tax	1,005	4,750
	Standard Deviation	1,581	3,500
$20,000–$25,000	Average Tax	3,362	7,469
	Standard Deviation	975	3,741
$25,000–$30,000	Average Tax	3,485	9,023
	Standard Deviation	2,251	3,778
$30,000–$35,000	Average Tax	912	7,961
	Standard Deviation	613	5,684
$35,000–$40,000	Average Tax	—	13,017
	Standard Deviation	—	4,336
$40,000–$45,000	Average Tax	—	15,284
	Standard Deviation	—	5,190
$45,000–$50,000	Average Tax	—	19,154
	Standard Deviation	—	4,865
$50,000–$55,000	Average Tax	—	22,194
	Standard Deviation	—	4,620
$55,000–$60,000	Average Tax	—	25,788
	Standard Deviation	—	5,286
$60,000–$65,000	Average Tax	—	28,345
	Standard Deviation	—	5,939
$65,000–$70,000	Average Tax	—	29,829
	Standard Deviation	—	6,590
$70,000–$75,000	Average Tax	—	30,630
	Standard Deviation	—	7,765
$75,000–$80,000	Average Tax	—	32,045
	Standard Deviation	—	8,341
$80,000–$90,000	Average Tax	—	35,302
	Standard Deviation	—	7,773
$90,000–$100,000	Average Tax	—	40,388
	Standard Deviation	—	9,861
$100,000 and over	Average Tax	—	78,088
	Standard Deviation	—	56,073
Column Total	Average Tax	1,104	18,318
	Standard Deviation	1,456	20,818

NOVA SCOTIA

Income Group		Below LICO	Equal to or above LICO
Under $10,000	Average Tax	$842	$2,334
	Standard Deviation	1,002	1,797
$10,000–$15,000	Average Tax	1,780	4,193
	Standard Deviation	1,681	1,423
$15,000–$20,000	Average Tax	1,461	4,530
	Standard Deviation	1,970	3,211
$20,000–$25,000	Average Tax	3,443	6,613
	Standard Deviation	2,235	3,588
$25,000–$30,000	Average Tax	4,650	7,875
	Standard Deviation	4,745	4,712
$30,000–$35,000	Average Tax	3,672	11,093
	Standard Deviation	—	4,596
$35,000–$40,000	Average Tax	—	15,033
	Standard Deviation	—	4,004
$40,000–$45,000	Average Tax	—	17,848
	Standard Deviation	—	4,889
$45,000–$50,000	Average Tax	—	20,384
	Standard Deviation	—	4,468
$50,000–$55,000	Average Tax	—	23,127
	Standard Deviation	—	5,418
$55,000–$60,000	Average Tax	—	25,875
	Standard Deviation	—	7,110
$60,000–$65,000	Average Tax	—	28,807
	Standard Deviation	—	7,061
$65,000–$70,000	Average Tax	—	30,816
	Standard Deviation	—	6,108
$70,000–$75,000	Average Tax	—	34,139
	Standard Deviation	—	6,618
$75,000–$80,000	Average Tax	—	38,793
	Standard Deviation	—	8,154
$80,000–$90,000	Average Tax	—	40,351
	Standard Deviation	—	8,356
$90,000–$100,000	Average Tax	—	45,469
	Standard Deviation	—	9,651
$100,000 and over	Average Tax	—	68,456
	Standard Deviation	—	27,805
Column Total	Average Tax	1,587	21,604
	Standard Deviation	2,034	18,587

NEW BRUNSWICK

Income Group		Below LICO	Equal to or above LICO
Under $10,000	Average Tax	$618	$3,249
	Standard Deviation	743	1,555
$10,000–$15,000	Average Tax	1,750	3,866
	Standard Deviation	1,940	1,948
$15,000–$20,000	Average Tax	1,360	4,579
	Standard Deviation	2,019	3,320
$20,000–$25,000	Average Tax	2,411	6,772
	Standard Deviation	2,673	3,426
$25,000–$30,000	Average Tax	6,378	9,211
	Standard Deviation	2,813	3,783
$30,000–$35,000	Average Tax	3,188	9,107
	Standard Deviation	3,022	6,057
$35,000–$40,000	Average Tax	—	13,197
	Standard Deviation	—	5,267
$40,000–$45,000	Average Tax	—	16,101
	Standard Deviation	—	5,813
$45,000–$50,000	Average Tax	—	18,975
	Standard Deviation	—	5,642
$50,000–$55,000	Average Tax	—	21,397
	Standard Deviation	—	6,715
$55,000–$60,000	Average Tax	—	25,917
	Standard Deviation	—	5,696
$60,000–$65,000	Average Tax	—	27,367
	Standard Deviation	—	7,817
$65,000–$70,000	Average Tax	—	31,097
	Standard Deviation	—	7,312
$70,000–$75,000	Average Tax	—	33,037
	Standard Deviation	—	6,705
$75,000–$80,000	Average Tax	—	34,216
	Standard Deviation	—	10,192
$80,000–$90,000	Average Tax	—	39,070
	Standard Deviation	—	9,018
$90,000–$100,000	Average Tax	—	44,985
	Standard Deviation	—	9,240
$100,000 and over	Average Tax	—	64,709
	Standard Deviation	—	33,278
Column Total	Average Tax	1,582	21,920
	Standard Deviation	2,185	18,641

QUEBEC

Income Group		Below LICO	Equal to or above LICO
Under $10,000	Average Tax	$628	$1,930
	Standard Deviation	1,034	2,077
$10,000–$15,000	Average Tax	2,395	4,627
	Standard Deviation	2,403	1,974
$15,000–$20,000	Average Tax	2,088	6,335
	Standard Deviation	2,537	2,732
$20,000–$25,000	Average Tax	1,915	8,754
	Standard Deviation	2,929	3,619
$25,000–$30,000	Average Tax	5,021	10,715
	Standard Deviation	4,313	4,216
$30,000–$35,000	Average Tax	3,460	12,045
	Standard Deviation	4,409	5,670
$35,000–$40,000	Average Tax	6,107	14,845
	Standard Deviation	5,058	6,001
$40,000–$45,000	Average Tax	4,361	19,169
	Standard Deviation	2,968	5,866
$45,000–$50,000	Average Tax	17,980	21,641
	Standard Deviation	6,075	5,218
$50,000–$55,000	Average Tax	4,071	25,357
	Standard Deviation	—	5,408
$55,000–$60,000	Average Tax	17,681	28,708
	Standard Deviation	6,508	5,671
$60,000–$65,000	Average Tax	—	30,833
	Standard Deviation	—	6,683
$65,000–$70,000	Average Tax	—	34,068
	Standard Deviation	—	7,504
$70,000–$75,000	Average Tax	—	37,467
	Standard Deviation	—	8,012
$75,000–$80,000	Average Tax	—	39,614
	Standard Deviation	—	8,046
$80,000–$90,000	Average Tax	—	43,940
	Standard Deviation	—	9,932
$90,000–$100,000	Average Tax	—	51,397
	Standard Deviation	—	9,113
$100,000 and over	Average Tax	—	79,836
	Standard Deviation	—	42,889
Column Total	Average Tax	2,024	27,421
	Standard Deviation	3,042	23,280

ONTARIO

Income Group			Below LICO	Equal to or above LICO
Under $10,000	Average Tax		$821	$4,592
	Standard Deviation		902	3,126
$10,000–$15,000	Average Tax		2,795	4,161
	Standard Deviation		1,935	2,876
$15,000–$20,000	Average Tax		2,618	4,891
	Standard Deviation		2,798	3,102
$20,000–$25,000	Average Tax		3,182	7,043
	Standard Deviation		3,301	3,525
$25,000–$30,000	Average Tax		7,229	10,090
	Standard Deviation		2,795	3,785
$30,000–$35,000	Average Tax		3,256	11,402
	Standard Deviation		4,155	5,176
$35,000–$40,000	Average Tax		9,462	14,879
	Standard Deviation		7,441	4,478
$40,000–$45,000	Average Tax		6,902	18,443
	Standard Deviation		—	4,785
$45,000–$50,000	Average Tax		8,339	20,311
	Standard Deviation		—	5,274
$50,000–$55,000	Average Tax		13,838	23,385
	Standard Deviation		1,233	5,000
$55,000–$60,000	Average Tax		9,879	25,035
	Standard Deviation		—	5,416
$60,000–$65,000	Average Tax		—	28,145
	Standard Deviation		—	6,299
$65,000–$70,000	Average Tax		—	30,964
	Standard Deviation		—	5,825
$70,000–$75,000	Average Tax		—	34,600
	Standard Deviation		—	7,412
$75,000–$80,000	Average Tax		—	35,929
	Standard Deviation		—	6,267
$80,000–$90,000	Average Tax		—	40,739
	Standard Deviation		—	8,429
$90,000–$100,000	Average Tax		—	44,202
	Standard Deviation		—	9,724
$100,000 and over	Average Tax		—	72,037
	Standard Deviation		—	33,580
Column Total	Average Tax		2,654	32,461
	Standard Deviation		3,153	26,274

MANITOBA

Income Group		Below LICO	Equal to or above LICO
Under $10,000	Average Tax	$785	$3,591
	Standard Deviation	797	—
$10,000–$15,000	Average Tax	2,750	4,352
	Standard Deviation	2,113	1,191
$15,000–$20,000	Average Tax	2,459	5,351
	Standard Deviation	2,088	2,918
$20,000–$25,000	Average Tax	3,155	7,129
	Standard Deviation	2,683	3,375
$25,000–$30,000	Average Tax	5,451	9,269
	Standard Deviation	2,747	3,478
$30,000–$35,000	Average Tax	4,452	10,999
	Standard Deviation	4,275	5,754
$35,000–$40,000	Average Tax	3,627	13,716
	Standard Deviation	1,882	4,616
$40,000–$45,000	Average Tax	7,833	16,307
	Standard Deviation	1,652	4,545
$45,000–$50,000	Average Tax	—	20,427
	Standard Deviation	—	6,460
$50,000–$55,000	Average Tax	—	22,508
	Standard Deviation	—	5,631
$55,000–$60,000	Average Tax	6,237	25,181
	Standard Deviation	1,103	6,218
$60,000–$65,000	Average Tax	—	26,641
	Standard Deviation	—	5,910
$65,000–$70,000	Average Tax	—	30,409
	Standard Deviation	—	7,932
$70,000–$75,000	Average Tax	—	31,535
	Standard Deviation	—	8,435
$75,000–$80,000	Average Tax	—	34,136
	Standard Deviation	—	8,270
$80,000–$90,000	Average Tax	—	38,665
	Standard Deviation	—	9,419
$90,000–$100,000	Average Tax	—	44,082
	Standard Deviation	—	10,116
$100,000 and over	Average Tax	—	68,474
	Standard Deviation	—	33,541
Column Total	Average Tax	2,474	25,405
	Standard Deviation	2,577	21,797

SASKATCHEWAN

Income Group		Below LICO	Equal to or above LICO
Under $10,000	Average Tax	$940	$6,535
	Standard Deviation	1019	440
$10,000–$15,000	Average Tax	2,667	4,639
	Standard Deviation	2,016	1231
$15,000–$20,000	Average Tax	2,508	6,405
	Standard Deviation	2,197	2,905
$20,000–$25,000	Average Tax	2,310	5,864
	Standard Deviation	2,403	3,855
$25,000–$30,000	Average Tax	5,499	10,061
	Standard Deviation	3,532	3,976
$30,000–$35,000	Average Tax	1,720	10,376
	Standard Deviation	1,651	5,717
$35,000–$40,000	Average Tax	6,366	12,775
	Standard Deviation	5,741	5,758
$40,000–$45,000	Average Tax	3,414	17,110
	Standard Deviation	1,819	4,776
$45,000–$50,000	Average Tax	4,808	20,301
	Standard Deviation	—	6,052
$50,000–$55,000	Average Tax	7,696	23,006
	Standard Deviation	—	5,985
$55,000–$60,000	Average Tax	7,129	26,487
	Standard Deviation	—	6,531
$60,000–$65,000	Average Tax	—	28,329
	Standard Deviation	—	6,814
$65,000–$70,000	Average Tax	—	32,334
	Standard Deviation	—	8,339
$70,000–$75,000	Average Tax	—	36,923
	Standard Deviation	—	8,177
$75,000–$80,000	Average Tax	—	38,957
	Standard Deviation	—	10,258
$80,000–$90,000	Average Tax	—	43,522
	Standard Deviation	—	12,705
$90,000–$100,000	Average Tax	—	48,911
	Standard Deviation	—	13,283
$100,000 and over	Average Tax	—	74,305
	Standard Deviation	—	34,600
Column Total	Average Tax	2,145	25,736
	Standard Deviation	2,398	23,047

ALBERTA

Income Group		Below LICO	Equal to or above LICO
Under $10,000	Average Tax	$821	$2,817
	Standard Deviation	917	—
$10,000–$15,000	Average Tax	2,305	4,144
	Standard Deviation	2,199	1,408
$15,000–$20,000	Average Tax	3,257	5,919
	Standard Deviation	3,382	2,307
$20,000–$25,000	Average Tax	2,578	6,266
	Standard Deviation	3,467	3,364
$25,000–$30,000	Average Tax	5,685	9,399
	Standard Deviation	3,954	3,557
$30,000–$35,000	Average Tax	7,448	11,373
	Standard Deviation	7,487	4,680
$35,000–$40,000	Average Tax	2,626	12,368
	Standard Deviation	2,512	5,927
$40,000–$45,000	Average Tax	5,309	15,801
	Standard Deviation	2,624	5,593
$45,000–$50,000	Average Tax	—	18,082
	Standard Deviation	—	5,502
$50,000–$55,000	Average Tax	—	20,882
	Standard Deviation	—	5,947
$55,000–$60,000	Average Tax	—	23,877
	Standard Deviation	—	6,308
$60,000–$65,000	Average Tax	—	26,644
	Standard Deviation	—	8,279
$65,000–$70,000	Average Tax	—	28,814
	Standard Deviation	—	8,116
$70,000–$75,000	Average Tax	10,503	31,375
	Standard Deviation	—	9,946
$75,000–$80,000	Average Tax	—	33,492
	Standard Deviation	—	8,169
$80,000–$90,000	Average Tax	—	39,257
	Standard Deviation	—	10,764
$90,000–$100,000	Average Tax	—	43,982
	Standard Deviation	—	12,357
$100,000 and over	Average Tax	—	74,122
	Standard Deviation	—	41,195
Column Total	Average Tax	2,548	28,164
	Standard Deviation	3,357	26,705

BRITISH COLUMBIA

Income Group		Below LICO	Equal to or above LICO
Under $10,000	Average Tax	$907	$2,672
	Standard Deviation	1,071	1,547
$10,000–$15,000	Average Tax	2,566	3,580
	Standard Deviation	1,936	1,627
$15,000–$20,000	Average Tax	2,753	5,699
	Standard Deviation	2,909	2,540
$20,000–$25,000	Average Tax	3,089	8,108
	Standard Deviation	3,174	3,616
$25,000–$30,000	Average Tax	7,019	10,078
	Standard Deviation	3,763	3,789
$30,000–$35,000	Average Tax	3,746	11,320
	Standard Deviation	4,265	5,176
$35,000–$40,000	Average Tax	7,711	14,497
	Standard Deviation	4,508	4,409
$40,000–$45,000	Average Tax	7,449	17,109
	Standard Deviation	—	4,209
$45,000–$50,000	Average Tax	6,412	21,062
	Standard Deviation	2,407	5,982
$50,000–$55,000	Average Tax	—	23,853
	Standard Deviation	—	5,607
$55,000–$60,000	Average Tax	—	25,677
	Standard Deviation	—	5,033
$60,000–$65,000	Average Tax	—	27,904
	Standard Deviation	—	6,021
$65,000–$70,000	Average Tax	—	30,209
	Standard Deviation	—	6,937
$70,000–$75,000	Average Tax	—	33,200
	Standard Deviation	—	7,631
$75,000–$80,000	Average Tax	—	36,419
	Standard Deviation	—	7,295
$80,000–$90,000	Average Tax	—	39,667
	Standard Deviation	—	7,179
$90,000–$100,000	Average Tax	—	46,297
	Standard Deviation	—	9,705
$100,000 and over	Average Tax	—	70,646
	Standard Deviation	—	30,712
Column Total	Average Tax	2,726	28,063
	Standard Deviation	3,067	22,464

Appendix Table A–4: Average tax paid by families by income group and family size for Canada and the provinces, 1992 (dollars)

CANADA

1 = 1 Member;
2 = 2 to 5 members;
3 = more than 5 members

Income Group		Family Size		
		1	**2**	**3**
Under $10,000	Average Tax	$756	$911	$932
	Standard Deviation	1,051	1,078	1,685
$10,000–$15,000	Average Tax	3,438	2,152	3,146
	Standard Deviation	2,081	2,134	2,615
$15,000–$20,000	Average Tax	3,085	4,074	1,995
	Standard Deviation	3,566	2,911	2,824
$20,000–$25,000	Average Tax	4,234	6,098	1,662
	Standard Deviation	4,242	3,594	2,658
$25,000–$30,000	Average Tax	10,246	8,196	6,225
	Standard Deviation	4,133	4,384	4,180
$30,000–$35,000	Average Tax	14,467	8,962	8,010
	Standard Deviation	4,052	5,721	4,298
$35,000–$40,000	Average Tax	17,799	12,593	10,971
	Standard Deviation	4,120	5,574	4,595
$40,000–$45,000	Average Tax	21,265	16,305	13,007
	Standard Deviation	4,527	5,485	4,436
$45,000–$50,000	Average Tax	24,300	19,507	15,666
	Standard Deviation	4,949	5,596	5,728
$50,000–$55,000	Average Tax	27,551	22,578	19,544
	Standard Deviation	5,017	5,993	6,275
$55,000–$60,000	Average Tax	29,721	25,617	23,197
	Standard Deviation	7,207	5,960	8,370
$60,000–$65,000	Average Tax	33,443	28,354	24,435
	Standard Deviation	6,879	7,033	6,618
$65,000–$70,000	Average Tax	37,334	31,057	23,860
	Standard Deviation	7,705	7,186	8,737

$70,000–$75,000	Average Tax	40,104	34,130	28,033
	Standard Deviation	10,662	7,794	1,0467
$75,000–$80,000	Average Tax	45,320	362,78	32,463
	Standard Deviation	9,879	7,903	9,328
$80,000–$90,000	Average Tax	51,090	41,150	32,809
	Standard Deviation	11,390	9,090	8,738
$90,000–$100,000	Average Tax	59,594	46,422	38,729
	Standard Deviation	12,896	10,201	11,612
$100,000 and over	Average Tax	84,135	71,355	62,061
	Standard Deviation	39,194	34,235	32,002
Column Total	Average Tax	12,024	24,405	22,967
	Standard Deviation	15,741	23,086	23,123

NEWFOUNDLAND

Income Group		Family Size 1	2	3
Under $10,000	Average Tax	$1,167	$1,143	$—
	Standard Deviation	1,389	1,756	—
$10,000–$15,000	Average Tax	2,852	1,318	11
	Standard Deviation	2,307	1,487	—
$15,000–$20,000	Average Tax	5,099	3,543	1,231
	Standard Deviation	4,513	2,999	1,168
$20,000–$25,000	Average Tax	1,129	5,411	3,064
	Standard Deviation	2,878	4,022	3,876
$25,000–$30,000	Average Tax	4,685	7,204	6,247
	Standard Deviation	5,987	4,402	4,359
$30,000–$35,000	Average Tax	12,344	8,965	4,696
	Standard Deviation	6,285	5,994	3,153
$35,000–$40,000	Average Tax	17,210	9,407	7,463
	Standard Deviation	5,621	6,483	4,428
$40,000–$45,000	Average Tax	25,558	12,754	9,968
	Standard Deviation	5,397	7,842	4,989
$45,000–$50,000	Average Tax	22,094	17,583	16,311
	Standard Deviation	6,876	7,456	6,495
$50,000–$55,000	Average Tax	26,822	21,362	17,375
	Standard Deviation	9,242	8,800	10,912
$55,000–$60,000	Average Tax	22,215	24,921	19,139
	Standard Deviation	7,320	9,293	9,909
$60,000–$65,000	Average Tax	41,151	28,317	20,140
	Standard Deviation	2,342	11,066	8,777
$65,000–$70,000	Average Tax	46,155	29,959	14,645
	Standard Deviation	—	11,924	7,368
$70,000–$75,000	Average Tax	—	31,788	23,007
	Standard Deviation	—	11,897	13,395
$75,000–$80,000	Average Tax	9,434	34,119	30,217
	Standard Deviation	—	12,600	15,395
$80,000–$90,000	Average Tax	—	40,466	30,015
	Standard Deviation	—	12,410	9,753
$90,000–$100,000	Average Tax	—	46,808	36,341
	Standard Deviation	—	11,666	19,910
$100,000 and over	Average Tax	62,036	67,240	59,838
	Standard Deviation	11,290	32,765	22,997
Column Total	Average Tax	8,306	17,895	19,640
	Standard Deviation	11,752	17,548	17,474

PRINCE EDWARD ISLAND

Income Group		Family Size		
		1	2	3
Under $10,000	Average Tax	$658	$1,125	$ —
	Standard Deviation	1,042	1,074	—
$10,000–$15,000	Average Tax	3,848	2,435	1,173
	Standard Deviation	2,465	2,497	—
$15,000–$20,000	Average Tax	1,626	4,089	917
	Standard Deviation	2,736	3,251	1,481
$20,000–$25,000	Average Tax	6,160	7,203	2,577
	Standard Deviation	4,704	2,780	—
$25,000–$30,000	Average Tax	11,420	7,584	5,929
	Standard Deviation	2,068	3,924	3,119
$30,000–$35,000	Average Tax	12,274	7,598	9,101
	Standard Deviation	5,949	5,552	3,461
$35,000–$40,000	Average Tax	14,987	12,956	12,107
	Standard Deviation	3,666	4,626	2,516
$40,000–$45,000	Average Tax	—	15,630	13,945
	Standard Deviation	—	5,343	3,576
$45,000–$50,000	Average Tax	23,168	18,767	—
	Standard Deviation	4,169	4,783	—
$50,000–$55,000	Average Tax	23,726	22,172	19,403
	Standard Deviation	—	5,029	3,122
$55,000–$60,000	Average Tax	31,631	25,268	20,700
	Standard Deviation	5,037	5,396	3,041
$60,000–$65,000	Average Tax	32,884	27,405	27,458
	Standard Deviation	—	6,856	1,120
$65,000–$70,000	Average Tax	—	30,948	22,403
	Standard Deviation	—	6,899	2,268
$70,000–$75,000	Average Tax	—	30,356	21,244
	Standard Deviation	—	8,129	—
$75,000–$80,000	Average Tax	—	32,598	29,005
	Standard Deviation	—	8,972	8,284
$80,000–$90,000	Average Tax	—	3,6267	27,837
	Standard Deviation	—	7,827	6,399
$90,000– $100,000	Average Tax	—	38,593	—
	Standard Deviation	—	10,118	—
$100,000 and over	Average Tax	100,771	79,297	59,449
	Standard Deviation	9,480	64,057	33,958
Column Total	Average Tax	8,257	17,444	19,069
	Standard Deviation	13,968	21,483	19,448

NOVA SCOTIA

Income Group		Family Size		
		1	2	3
Under $10,000	Average Tax	$861	$757	$228
	Standard Deviation	1,177	906	357
$10,000–$15,000	Average Tax	2,941	2,162	1,635
	Standard Deviation	2,222	1,801	2,874
$15,000–$20,000	Average Tax	2,141	3,926	310
	Standard Deviation	3,007	2,776	537
$20,000–$25,000	Average Tax	6,087	5,651	2,640
	Standard Deviation	3,249	3,734	1,781
$25,000–$30,000	Average Tax	10,196	6,690	8,830
	Standard Deviation	3,979	4,917	3,924
$30,000–$35,000	Average Tax	13,744	10,424	10,973
	Standard Deviation	3,623	4,506	2,576
$35,000–$40,000	Average Tax	17,892	14,532	12,866
	Standard Deviation	2,599	3,981	2,186
$40,000–$45,000	Average Tax	21,633	17,483	16,920
	Standard Deviation	3,000	4,652	1,207
$45,000–$50,000	Average Tax	24,882	20,049	13,686
	Standard Deviation	1,674	4,274	8,576
$50,000–$55,000	Average Tax	28,112	22,609	22,819
	Standard Deviation	3,652	5,252	5,301
$55,000–$60,000	Average Tax	32,447	25,395	22,444
	Standard Deviation	8,004	6,202	9,593
$60,000–$65,000	Average Tax	35,817	27,680	25,552
	Standard Deviation	144	7,032	7,884
$65,000–$70,000	Average Tax	36,288	30,828	28,492
	Standard Deviation	—	6,087	4,625
$70,000–$75,000	Average Tax	39,483	34,039	33,198
	Standard Deviation	4,103	6,942	3,131
$75,000–$80,000	Average Tax	46,608	37,900	28,898
	Standard Deviation	676	8,065	8,506
$80,000–$90,000	Average Tax	—	40,206	36,909
	Standard Deviation	—	9,066	11,638
$90,000–$100,000	Average Tax	49,211	44,875	35,782
	Standard Deviation	1,827	9,362	10,430
$100,000 and over	Average Tax	73,548	67,259	51,203
	Standard Deviation	33,223	26,911	11,476
Column Total	Average Tax	7,704	18,343	20,155
	Standard Deviation	11,423	17,499	16,236

NEW BRUNSWICK

Income Group		Family Size		
		1	2	3
Under $10,000	Average Tax	$506	$610	$51
	Standard Deviation	890	749	—
$10,000–$15,000	Average Tax	3,846	1,633	—
	Standard Deviation	1,854	1,891	—
$15,000–$20,000	Average Tax	1,941	3,666	1,262
	Standard Deviation	2,935	3,111	1,602
$20,000–$25,000	Average Tax	4,783	5,719	1,094
	Standard Deviation	4,121	3,406	425
$25,000–$30,000	Average Tax	9,535	8,722	—
	Standard Deviation	4,372	3,682	—
$30,000–$35,000	Average Tax	15,315	7,737	6,402
	Standard Deviation	2,992	6,025	6,315
$35,000–$40,000	Average Tax	18,229	12,226	13,293
	Standard Deviation	2,678	5,270	3,753
$40,000–$45,000	Average Tax	21,127	16,068	5,752
	Standard Deviation	4,336	5,616	—
$45,000–$50,000	Average Tax	22,588	18,777	13,456
	Standard Deviation	6,394	5,265	7,724
$50,000–$55,000	Average Tax	28,257	21,614	16,325
	Standard Deviation	3,041	6,521	7,648
$55,000–$60,000	Average Tax	30,760	25,998	26,128
	Standard Deviation	7,987	5,620	4,541
$60,000–$65,000	Average Tax	37,732	27,378	22,904
	Standard Deviation	8,873	7,286	9,694
$65,000–$70,000	Average Tax	39,496	30,649	25,533
	Standard Deviation	5,377	7,286	8,090
$70,000–$75,000	Average Tax	38,387	32,964	31,542
	Standard Deviation	1,296	7,315	4,116
$75,000–$80,000	Average Tax	43,557	35,021	18,839
	Standard Deviation	123	8,702	8,083
$80,000–$90,000	Average Tax	—	40,096	31,880
	Standard Deviation	—	9,345	5,322
$90,000–$100,000	Average Tax	54,350	45,216	36,845
	Standard Deviation	—	9,364	9,644
$100,000 and over	Average Tax	76,337	63,059	80,446
	Standard Deviation	11,285	27,678	91,883
Column Total	Average Tax	9,748	19,439	25,899
	Standard Deviation	12,940	18,148	35,914

QUEBEC

Income Group		Family Size		
		1	2	3
Under $10,000	Average Tax	$548	$1,013	$1,170
	Standard Deviation	929	1,160	2,183
$10,000–$15,000	Average Tax	3,695	1,842	4,084
	Standard Deviation	2,087	2,341	2,766
$15,000–$20,000	Average Tax	3,023	3,906	1,199
	Standard Deviation	3,818	2,915	2,681
$20,000–$25,000	Average Tax	4,717	6,497	621
	Standard Deviation	5,024	3,810	1,665
$25,000–$30,000	Average Tax	11,584	8,799	7,539
	Standard Deviation	4,024	4,708	5,797
$30,000–$35,000	Average Tax	15,615	9,484	6,569
	Standard Deviation	4,505	5,944	5,130
$35,000–$40,000	Average Tax	18,754	13,690	10,473
	Standard Deviation	4,960	5,740	6,561
$40,000–$45,000	Average Tax	23,543	17,557	15,494
	Standard Deviation	4,802	5,563	6,164
$45,000–$50,000	Average Tax	26,304	21,150	15,944
	Standard Deviation	3,516	5,470	4,860
$50,000–$55,000	Average Tax	26,154	24,477	21,867
	Standard Deviation	4,751	6,307	2,491
$55,000–$60,000	Average Tax	30,317	28,085	28,319
	Standard Deviation	8,131	5,734	11,833
$60,000–$65,000	Average Tax	36,597	30,791	27,615
	Standard Deviation	3,771	7,019	5,176
$65,000–$70,000	Average Tax	36,041	33,893	25,955
	Standard Deviation	8,646	7,186	13,124
$70,000–$75,000	Average Tax	41,260	36,674	30,245
	Standard Deviation	8,137	7,938	10,140
$75,000–$80,000	Average Tax	42,488	39,359	32,327
	Standard Deviation	6,419	8,786	18,752
$80,000–$90,000	Average Tax	48,762	43,980	31,958
	Standard Deviation	11,305	9,132	8,814
$90,000– $100,000	Average Tax	49,416	50,903	33,493
	Standard Deviation	13,927	9,203	15,619
$100,000 and over	Average Tax	95,687	72,935	57,078
	Standard Deviation	59,985	35,866	26,085
Column Total	Average Tax	10,725	23,494	14,555
	Standard Deviation	14,783	21,096	18,953

ONTARIO

Income Group		Family Size		
		1	2	3
Under $10,000	Average Tax	$769	$958	$967
	Standard Deviation	1,068	1,109	1,217
$10,000–$15,000	Average Tax	3,490	2,461	4,497
	Standard Deviation	2,132	2,258	869
$15,000–$20,000	Average Tax	2,851	4,468	2,587
	Standard Deviation	3,272	2,839	3,426
$20,000–$25,000	Average Tax	4,289	6,244	4,862
	Standard Deviation	3,998	3,706	3,613
$25,000–$30,000	Average Tax	10,620	8,862	6,695
	Standard Deviation	3,388	4,264	3,134
$30,000–$35,000	Average Tax	14,245	9,405	10,234
	Standard Deviation	3,370	5,791	3,159
$35,000–$40,000	Average Tax	17,935	13,597	12,761
	Standard Deviation	3,344	4,891	2,426
$40,000–$45,000	Average Tax	21,178	17,357	14,506
	Standard Deviation	3,618	4,430	2,792
$45,000–$50,000	Average Tax	23,910	19,494	17,693
	Standard Deviation	4,769	5,072	6,131
$50,000–$55,000	Average Tax	27,537	22,533	20,511
	Standard Deviation	4,860	4,768	5,689
$55,000–$60,000	Average Tax	30,059	24,946	23,626
	Standard Deviation	5,426	4,997	6,238
$60,000–$65,000	Average Tax	32,117	28,223	27,155
	Standard Deviation	6,170	6,011	3,243
$65,000–$70,000	Average Tax	37,244	30,709	28,192
	Standard Deviation	5,530	5,597	6,252
$70,000–$75,000	Average Tax	40,973	34,001	31,108
	Standard Deviation	12,199	6,490	10,772
$75,000–$80,000	Average Tax	45,104	36,023	35,708
	Standard Deviation	8,198	5,373	4,713
$80,000–$90,000	Average Tax	48,577	41,044	33,364
	Standard Deviation	10,368	7,592	8,525
$90,000– $100,000	Average Tax	60,123	46,154	38,119
	Standard Deviation	10,558	8,821	10,894
$100,000 and over	Average Tax	83,832	71,982	63,598
	Standard Deviation	35,705	32,970	21,374
Column Total	Average Tax	14,959	29,625	30,509
	Standard Deviation	18,104	25,596	23,445

MANITOBA

Income Group		Family Size		
		1	2	3
Under $10,000	Average Tax	$701	$771	$516
	Standard Deviation	806	918	415
$10,000–$15,000	Average Tax	4,094	2,379	2,620
	Standard Deviation	1,749	2,059	3,580
$15,000–$20,000	Average Tax	2,889	4,038	7,424
	Standard Deviation	3,247	2,691	7,648
$20,000–$25,000	Average Tax	3,986	6,318	3,693
	Standard Deviation	3,799	3,312	2,524
$25,000–$30,000	Average Tax	9,689	7,960	5,574
	Standard Deviation	3,771	3,446	3,057
$30,000–$35,000	Average Tax	15,224	7,134	10,630
	Standard Deviation	2,655	5,511	4,893
$35,000–$40,000	Average Tax	17,955	12,171	11,514
	Standard Deviation	3,279	4,978	6,267
$40,000–$45,000	Average Tax	19,560	15,307	9,137
	Standard Deviation	3,822	4,432	3,210
$45,000–$50,000	Average Tax	26,997	18,552	13,608
	Standard Deviation	4,503	5,559	5,133
$50,000–$55,000	Average Tax	29,116	21,398	17,588
	Standard Deviation	4,710	5,549	6,077
$55,000–$60,000	Average Tax	27,866	24,645	18,242
	Standard Deviation	9,455	6,545	6,228
$60,000–$65,000	Average Tax	28,339	26,709	22,354
	Standard Deviation	13,071	5,854	4,708
$65,000–$70,000	Average Tax	42,862	29,042	28,092
	Standard Deviation	1,947	7,132	—
$70,000–$75,000	Average Tax	29,213	33,136	21,384
	Standard Deviation	11,568	8,841	11,649
$75,000–$80,000	Average Tax	43,754	33,991	34,571
	Standard Deviation	4,911	9,311	3,414
$80,000–$90,000	Average Tax	49,504	39,415	34,875
	Standard Deviation	5,431	8,861	9,387
$90,000–$100,000	Average Tax	—	44,815	45,290
	Standard Deviation	—	11,217	8,240
$100,000 and over	Average Tax	71,710	65,702	57,505
	Standard Deviation	45,031	32,312	24,185
Column Total	Average Tax	10,241	22,153	23,693
	Standard Deviation	12,329	20,797	19,910

SASKATCHEWAN

Income Group		Family Size		
		1	**2**	**3**
Under $10,000	Average Tax	$996	$932	$356
	Standard Deviation	1,301	1,042	436
$10,000–$15,000	Average Tax	3,945	2,634	6,009
	Standard Deviation	1,716	2,125	—
$15,000–$20,000	Average Tax	4,875	4,485	2,433
	Standard Deviation	3,793	3,068	1,751
$20,000–$25,000	Average Tax	3,573	5,980	798
	Standard Deviation	3,847	3,083	1,031
$25,000–$30,000	Average Tax	10,535	8,651	6,028
	Standard Deviation	3,772	4,319	3,155
$30,000–$35,000	Average Tax	15,046	8,518	6,772
	Standard Deviation	3,756	5,583	3,739
$35,000–$40,000	Average Tax	17,959	11,754	9,363
	Standard Deviation	3,876	6,131	4,029
$40,000–$45,000	Average Tax	22,047	16,237	12,637
	Standard Deviation	5,512	4,348	4,900
$45,000–$50,000	Average Tax	23,824	19,789	15,374
	Standard Deviation	5,675	5,952	7,451
$50,000–$55,000	Average Tax	28,826	22,755	19,163
	Standard Deviation	5,132	5,886	8,436
$55,000–$60,000	Average Tax	28,509	25,943	23,267
	Standard Deviation	11,101	6,506	4,653
$60,000–$65,000	Average Tax	31,629	28,412	26,578
	Standard Deviation	7,149	6,884	8,991
$65,000–$70,000	Average Tax	42,519	31,734	30,896
	Standard Deviation	4,671	8,836	3,730
$70,000–$75,000	Average Tax	44,889	36,011	25,839
	Standard Deviation	13,850	6,333	15,420
$75,000–$80,000	Average Tax	55,474	37,311	34,608
	Standard Deviation	9,150	8,348	9,729
$80,000–$90,000	Average Tax	61,894	43,209	28,001
	Standard Deviation	12,602	11,776	12,043
$90,000–$100,000	Average Tax	82,051	48,773	46,664
	Standard Deviation	—	13,183	8,174
$100,000 and over	Average Tax	92,193	73,421	54,968
	Standard Deviation	45,645	30,685	25,883
Column Total	Average Tax	12,156	23,776	20,718
	Standard Deviation	17,676	23,029	19,215

ALBERTA

Income Group		Family Size		
		1	2	3
Under $10,000	Average Tax	$986	$871	$567
	Standard Deviation	941	933	364
$10,000–$15,000	Average Tax	2,856	2,505	269
	Standard Deviation	2,388	2,046	—
$15,000–$20,000	Average Tax	6,251	3,993	4,650
	Standard Deviation	3,873	2,887	1,985
$20,000–$25,000	Average Tax	3,354	5,583	5,409
	Standard Deviation	3,950	3,349	1,933
$25,000–$30,000	Average Tax	9,050	7,542	4,642
	Standard Deviation	4,415	3,798	5,194
$30,000–$35,000	Average Tax	12,907	10,017	7,204
	Standard Deviation	5,240	5,069	4,190
$35,000–$40,000	Average Tax	16,463	10,014	5,155
	Standard Deviation	6,110	6,003	5,767
$40,000–$45,000	Average Tax	18,828	14,530	12,193
	Standard Deviation	5,282	5,949	2,786
$45,000–$50,000	Average Tax	23,204	17,824	14,057
	Standard Deviation	5,468	5,860	3,083
$50,000–$55,000	Average Tax	27,216	20,749	20,139
	Standard Deviation	5,757	6,073	5,689
$55,000–$60,000	Average Tax	28,413	23,571	25,082
	Standard Deviation	8,747	5,871	5,272
$60,000–$65,000	Average Tax	34,680	26,607	21,867
	Standard Deviation	9,063	8,472	4,634
$65,000–$70,000	Average Tax	35,094	28,439	20,733
	Standard Deviation	14,278	7,634	2,864
$70,000–$75,000	Average Tax	32,645	32,738	21,426
	Standard Deviation	5,775	9,793	10,916
$75,000–$80,000	Average Tax	44,039	33,181	26,932
	Standard Deviation	420	8,228	2,858
$80,000–$90,000	Average Tax	53,120	38,911	34,418
	Standard Deviation	10,950	11,002	4,426
$90,000– $100,000	Average Tax	65,068	44,505	43,405
	Standard Deviation	21,211	12,660	7,825
$100,000 and over	Average Tax	82,014	73,681	76,760
	Standard Deviation	42,772	42,081	54,950
Column Total	Average Tax	12,235	25,013	27,819
	Standard Deviation	15,651	26,873	34,250

BRITISH COLUMBIA

Income Group		Family Size		
		1	**2**	**3**
Under $10,000	Average Tax	$814	$1,060	$1,326
	Standard Deviation	1,045	1,228	723
$10,000–$15,000	Average Tax	2,971	2,155	1,242
	Standard Deviation	1,326	1,922	1,708
$15,000–$20,000	Average Tax	3,899	3,970	2,502
	Standard Deviation	3,470	2,799	2,655
$20,000–$25,000	Average Tax	4,600	6,393	51
	Standard Deviation	4,334	3,436	—
$25,000–$30,000	Average Tax	10,709	8,461	410
	Standard Deviation	3,605	3,921	—
$30,000–$35,000	Average Tax	14,834	8,014	7,351
	Standard Deviation	3,157	5,562	4,397
$35,000–$40,000	Average Tax	17,220	12,511	9,914
	Standard Deviation	3,531	4,907	1,684
$40,000–$45,000	Average Tax	19,806	16,080	13,068
	Standard Deviation	3,134	4,414	2,865
$45,000–$50,000	Average Tax	23,573	19,544	15,925
	Standard Deviation	5,128	5,028	4,268
$50,000–$55,000	Average Tax	27,633	22,482	17,849
	Standard Deviation	4,901	5,526	4,798
$55,000–$60,000	Average Tax	30,287	25,659	22,989
	Standard Deviation	5,896	4,423	3,866
$60,000–$65,000	Average Tax	34,061	27,430	25,560
	Standard Deviation	4,106	5,627	8,772
$65,000–$70,000	Average Tax	35,053	30,705	23,441
	Standard Deviation	2,192	5,766	7,152
$70,000–$75,000	Average Tax	44,120	33,503	28,773
	Standard Deviation	6,020	7,413	672
$75,000–$80,000	Average Tax	43,057	36,310	33,216
	Standard Deviation	15,487	6,376	7,643
$80,000–$90,000	Average Tax	49,463	40,374	34,830
	Standard Deviation	9,838	7,158	7,740
$90,000–$100,000	Average Tax	62,576	44,406	28,766
	Standard Deviation	6,687	9,526	12,866
$100,000 and over	Average Tax	75,539	70,338	54,468
	Standard Deviation	26,490	30,335	16,186
Column Total	Average Tax	12,760	25,553	26,572
	Standard Deviation	13,952	22,683	19,332

Glossary

Some of the principal terms, measures, and concepts in *Tax Facts 8*

About indices

Index: a method of measuring the percentage changes from a base year of a certain item, such as the price, volume, or value of food, or the dollar amount of taxes. In order to construct an Index, the price, volume, or value of the particular item being indexed in each year is divided by the price, volume, or value of the item in the base year; then multiplied by 100. An index has a value of 100 in the base year; in this book the base year is 1961.

Consumer Price Index: measures the percentage change from a base year in the cost of purchasing a constant "basket" of goods and services representing the purchases by a particular population group in a specified time period. The Consumer Price Index or CPI, as it is often called, reflects price movements of some 300 items. The CPI is calculated monthly by Statistics Canada (see below).

Consumer Tax Index: measures the percentage change from a base year in the average Canadian family's tax bill. The Consumer

Tax Index, or CTI, is composed of federal, provincial, and municipal taxes. The CTI, calculated by The Fraser Institute, was introduced by the Institute for the first time in Edition One, *How Much Tax Do You Really Pay?*

Balanced Budget Tax Index: is the same as the Consumer Tax Index except that included in the calculation is the amount of tax that would have to be raised if governments did not issue debt and were in fact balancing their budgets. This index was introduced by The Fraser Institute for the first time in Edition Two, *Tax Facts.*

Some statistical terms

Statistics Canada: is Canada's official statistical agency which is often referred to as "StatsCan." Statistics Canada provided much of the published and unpublished data for this book. For a detailed listing of these sources, see the Bibliography.

Average Canadian Family: represents a family that had average income in a particular year. The averages were constructed from Statistics Canada's Survey of Consumer Finances, details of which appear in the Bibliography.

Family Expenditure Survey: refers to the Statistics Canada surveys which show patterns of family expenditure for Canada by selected characteristics such as urban and/or rural area, family type, life cycle, income, age of head, tenure, occupation of head, education of head, country of origin and, if applicable, immigrant arrival year. The tables in these surveys which were integral to this book were those entitled, "Detailed Average Expenditure by Family Income for All Families and Unattached Individuals." From these tables it was possible to look at the spending patterns of the average family in each income class.

Family: refers to a group of persons dependent upon a common or pooled income for their major expenditure items and living in the same dwelling. The term also applies to a financially independent unattached individual living alone.

Shelter Expenditure: is included as one of the selected expenditure items in this book. It refers to expenditures on rented or owned living quarters on repairs to these quarters; on mortgage interest and on other housing, such as vacation homes, lodging at university or at remote work locations. It also includes expenditures on water and heating fuel.

Survey of Consumer Finances: refers to Statistics Canada's survey which details families' incomes and family characteristics. Information is given on head and spouse incomes (such as salaries, wages, and pension), residence (province, rural/urban), personal characteristics (family size, age, education level, and so forth) and labour-related characteristics (occupation, employment status, etc).

Income concepts used in the book

Cash Income: is the income that a family would report when completing a government survey, such as the Family Expenditure Survey, Survey of Consumer Finances, or the Census form. It includes income that one receives regularly, such as salary or wage income (before tax) and payments from government such as family allowances. Families generally underreport their income so cash income estimates used in this study are adjusted to include income that is often omitted when a family speaks of its income. Income which is often excluded is bond or bank interest and dividend income.

Income from Government: is income that a family receives as payment from the government, whereas taxes are payments to the government. Therefore, income from the government can be considered a "negative tax." It is often referred to as a transfer payment. It includes such items as family allowance payments, old age security payments, veterans' grants, etc.

Hidden Income: is income that a family receives but probably does not consider to be a part of its income. Hidden income is largely made up of employer contributions to pension plans, medical premiums, and insurance plans. Another example is imputed non-farm rent. (For a more complete discussion of imputed non-farm rent see The Fraser Institute publication *Rent Control— A Popular Paradox*, p. 33).

Hidden Purchasing Power Loss: the prices of articles that the family buys are higher by the amount of hidden taxes which are paid to government by an intermediary and not at the point of final sale. For example, sales taxes paid by the manufacturer are typically added to the price charged to the wholesaler or retailer and are accordingly built into the final sales price but not called a tax. Therefore, the consumer actually loses purchasing power by the amount of these taxes. In this book the purchasing power loss has been given back to the family as one of the components of total income before tax.

Total Income Before Tax: is the term used in this book to designate the amount of income the family would have received before paying tax. It is composed of cash income which includes income from government (transfer payments), hidden income, and hidden purchasing power loss.

Deciles: all families were lined up according to total income before tax from lowest to highest and then divided into ten groups, i.e. the first decile contains the first 10 percent of families, etc.

Transfer Payments: see "Income from Government" in this section.

About taxes

Tax Burden: is the means of determining who ultimately pays tax and is synonymous with the term "tax incidence." Tax burden is measured by the decline in real purchasing power that results from the imposition of a tax.

Balanced Budget Tax Rate: is the tax rate that Canadians would face if governments had to balance their budgets and finance all expenditures from current tax revenue instead of issuing debt.

Deferred Taxation: the debt incurred by the various levels of government to finance the expenditures that cannot be met by current tax revenue is, in effect, deferred taxation because the debts and interest on them must ultimately be paid out of future tax revenue.

Direct Taxes: are taxes which are paid directly by the family. Examples of direct taxes are the personal income tax and provincial retail sales taxes. They are often referred to as explicit taxes.

Hidden Taxes: are taxes that are concealed in the price of articles that one buys. Hidden taxes are also referred to as implicit taxes. The most well-known form of the hidden tax is the indirect tax. Examples of hidden taxes are the tobacco tax, manufacturers' sales taxes and import duties.

Social Security Taxes: are composed of both federal and provincial taxes. The federal category includes contributions to Unemployment Insurance. Provincial Social Security taxes include employer and employee contributions to Workers' Compensation and Industrial Employees' Vacations. Also included in this category as taxes are payments to the Canada and Quebec Pension Plans and Medical and Hospital Insurance Premiums.

Corporate Profits Tax: is the tax paid on the profits of a corporation.

Progressive, Proportional, and Regressive Taxation: are terms which refer to the proportionality of taxes on income. A tax is called proportional if it takes the same fraction of income from low income people as it does from high income people. (Unemployment Insurance payments and Canada Pension payments up to the maximum earnings level are examples of proportional taxes). A progressive tax is one that takes a greater proportion of income from high-income earners than from those with low incomes (income tax, for example). A regressive tax is one that takes a greater proportion of income from low income people than it does from high income people (sales tax, for example).

Negative Tax: see "Income from Government" in the previous section.

Taxation Powers Under the Constitution of Canada: the general scheme of taxation in the British North America Act might be summarized in this way:

1. the federal government is given an unlimited power to tax.
2. the provinces are also given what amounts to an unlimited power to tax "within the province," that is to say, an unlim-

ited power to tax persons within their jurisdiction and to impose taxes in respect to property located and income earned within the province. (They may not, however, levy indirect taxes). But their taxing powers are framed in such a way as to preclude them from imposing taxes which would have the effect of creating barriers to interprovincial trade, and generally from taxing persons and property outside the province.

Bibliography

Selected sources

Bird, Richard M., *Growth of Government Spending in Canada*, Canadian Tax Foundation, July 1970.

Browning, Edgar K., "The Burden of Taxation," *Journal of Political Economy*, Vol. 86, No. 4, August 1978.

Browning, Edgar K. and William R. Johnson, *The Distribution of the Tax Burden*, American Enterprise Institute, 1979.

Burrows, Marie, *Fiscal Positions of the Provinces: The 1983 Budgets*, Conference Board of Canada, Aeric, 1983.

Campbell, Harry F., "An Input-Output Analysis of the Commodity Structure of Indirect Taxes in Canada," *The Canadian Journal of Economics*, August 1975, p. 433.

Canadian Tax Foundation, *The National Finances—An Analysis of the Revenues and Expenditures of the Government of Canada, 1991*, Canadian Tax Foundation, 1992.

———, *Provincial and Municipal Finances, 1989*, Canadian Tax Foundation, 1985.

Conference Board of Canada, *Provincial Outlook*, Winter 1991, Vol. 6, No. 1, Aeric.

———, *Provincial Outlook*, March 1992, Vol. 7, No. 1, Aeric.

Dodge, David A., "Impact of Tax, Transfer and Expenditure Policies of Government on the Distribution of Personal Incomes in Canada," *The Review of Income and Wealth*, Series 21, No. 1, March 1975, pp. 1-52.

Gillespie, W. Irwin, *Incidence of Taxes and Public Expenditures in the Canadian Economy*, Studies of the Royal Commission on Taxation, No. 2, 1966.

———, *In Search of Robin Hood*, C.D. Howe Research Institute, 1978.

Goffman, Irving J., *The Burden of Canadian Taxation*, Tax Paper No. 29, Canadian Tax Foundation, July 1972.

Horry, Isabella D., Sally C. Pipes and Michael A. Walker, *Tax Facts 7*, The Fraser Institute, 1990.

International Monetary Fund, *International Financial Statistics, Yearbook 1991*, Washington D.C., 1991.

Marx, Karl and Friedrich Engels, *Manifesto of the Communist Party*, 1848.

Maslove, Allan M., *The Pattern of Taxation in Canada*, Economic Council of Canada, December 1972.

Meerman, Jacob P., "The Definition of Income in Studies of Budget Incidence and Income Distribution," *Review of Income and Wealth*, Series 20, No. 4, December 1974, pp. 512-22.

Musgrave, Richard A., and Peggy B. Musgrave, *Public Finance in Theory and Practice*, McGraw-Hill, Inc., 1973.

O.E.C.D., *Agricultural Policies, Markets and Trade, Monitoring and Outlook 1992*, Paris 1992.

———, *Revenue Statistics of O.E.C.D. Member Countries 1965-1991*, Paris 1991.

Pechman, Joseph A., and Benjamin A. Okner, *Who Bears the Tax Burden?* Studies of Government Finance, The Brookings Institute, 1974.

Pipes, Sally C., and Michael A. Walker, *Tax Facts 6*, The Fraser Institute, 1988.

———, *Tax Facts 5*, The Fraser Institute, 1986.

———, *Tax Facts 4*, The Fraser Institute, 1984.

_____, *Tax Facts 3*, The Fraser Institute, 1982.

_____, *Tax Facts*, The Fraser Institute, 1979.

Star, Spencer and Sally C. Pipes, *Income and Taxation in Canada 1961-1975*, The Fraser Institute, 1977.

Walker, Michael, ed., Thomas Courchene, Perrin Lewis, Pierre Lortie, et al., *Canadian Conference at the Crossroads: The Search for a Federal-Provincial Balance*, The Fraser Institute, 1979.

Walker, Michael, ed., *How Much Tax Do You Really Pay?*, The Fraser Institute, 1976.

Walker, Michael, ed., David Laidler, Michael Parkin, Jackson Grayson, et al., *The Illusion of Wage and Price Control*, The Fraser Institute, 1976.

Walker, Michael and G. Campbell Watkins, editors, *Oil in the Seventies*, The Fraser Institute, 1977.

Wonnacott, Ronald J. and P. Wonnacott, *Free Trade Between the United States and Canada*, Harvard University Press, 1967.